A Step By Step Introduction To 8080 Microprocessor Systems

David L. Cohn and James L. Melsa

Department of Electrical Engineering
University of Notre Dame

dilithium
PRESS
P.O. Box 92   Forest Grove, Oregon 97116

A Step By Step Introduction To 8080 Microprocessor Systems

David L. Cohn
James L. Melsa

Department of Electrical Engineering
University of Notre Dame

ISBN 0-918398-04-5

Library of Congress Cataloging in Publication Data

Cohn, David L   1943-
    A step by step introduction to 8080 microprocessor
systems.

    1. INTEL 8080 (Computer) 2. Microprocessors.
I. Melsa, James L., joint author. II. Title.
QA76.8.I28C63   001.6'4'04   77-21762
ISBN 0-918398-04-5

Printed In The United States of America

To our own eight bits:

Alan
Elisabeth
Jennifer
Jon
Laina
Mark
Peter
Susan

A Step By Step Introduction
To 8080 Microprocessor Systems

CONTENTS

PREFACE

This microprocessor book is written for people who don't know anything about microprocessors but who wish they did. The step-by-step presentation does not require any computer or electronics background; so anyone who is interested can follow it. However, the book is not only intended for beginners. Engineers and technicians who are familiar with electronics will find the software descriptions valuable in updating their skills. Computer professionals will find the detailed treatment of the 8080 architecture and instruction set useful.

The best way to learn about any type of computer is to sit down and use it. For those readers lucky enough to have access to an 8080 system, the book contains a number of exercises which illustrate the concepts discussed in each chapter. If at all possible, these exercises should be done while the book is being read.

Of course, many readers will not have an 8080-based computer. Indeed, they may be trying to decide if they should buy such a system. Therefore, many of the exercises have been designed to be worked out with pencil and paper. If the easy exercises at the front of the book are done carefully, the material later in the book will also be easy.

In order to present a clear picture of microprocessors, this book focuses on one particular type of device, the 8080. By concentrating on the 8080, the details of microprocessor structure can be examined. When the reader fully understands the 8080, he will be amazed at how easy it is to understand other types of microprocessors. The same approach is used when describing system programs. These programs are very useful for writing and fixing other pro-

grams and they are described in detail. Most of the discu
sion is general and the INTEL software products are used i
the examples. As with the processors, once a user unde
stands one assembler or editor, it is easy to figure out ho
others work.

This book is intended as an introduction, not as a con
plete instruction manual. It has been written to teach th
concepts of microprocessors, not to present all of the de
tails. We have tried to insure that everything that is in th
book is correct but a number of minor things have bee
omitted. The guiding philosophy is to prepare the reader t
understand the manufacturer's instruction manual tha
accompanies whatever microcomputer he might use.

In any project of this sort, many people contribute in var
ous large and small ways. The authors would like to expres
their appreciation to their colleagues and students who pro
vided many helpful suggestions. In particular, Dr. James L
Massey should be recognized for his detailed and construc
tive review of the manuscript. The leadership of Dea
Joseph C. Hogan of the College of Engineering at Notr
Dame has provided the atmosphere which made this effor
possible and also deserves special attention.

David L. Cohn
James L. Melsa

South Bend, Indiana

INTRODUCTION

.1 Historical Perspectives

hroughout the history of its development, solid state tech-
ology has been directed toward reducing the size and
veight of devices required to perform various tasks. In the
early days, this meant that the size of discrete transistors
became smaller. Soon it became possible to put a number
of functions inside one integrated circuit package. Initially
his meant a single gate or several gates were made at one
ime; later, a number of functions were accommodated in a
single package. Recently, it became evident that very com-
olex functions could be built in one package.

This led to the development of elaborate systems to design custom integrated circuit chips. Sophisticated computer programs to reduce a logic diagram to an integrated
circuit have been written. Several examples of the end product of this technique are calculator chips, UARTs, digital
watches, and other common large volume products. It soon
became apparent, however, that many applications did not
require the volume that would justify a custom large scale
integrated circuit. In 1971, the INTEL Corporation decided to
try to build a general purpose integrated circuit that could
be used by several different customers. They adopted the
approach used by the computer industry: a stored program
machine. The central element of this system was a chip
which performed the primary functions of the central
processing unit of a computer. This quickly became known
as the "computer on a chip" or the microprocessor.

The CPU chip needed a number of support chips to provide timing, memory, and input/output interfacing. Thus, a
single chip was nowhere near enough to do anything useful.

However, the overall system concept was very successful.

Since that time, a number of manufacturers have developed and are selling a large number of different types of microprocessors. Most microprocessors still require a number of support chips in order to function. However some manufacturers have recently announced complete one-chip computers.

1.2 Typical Applications

Microprocessors have been used in a vast range of applications. Frequently they are used to replace the large number of integrated circuits which would be required if more traditional hardwired logic design methods are used.

There are several properties microprocessor applications tend to have in common. In general, microprocessors can be viewed as replacements for hardwired logic. There are some situations where they have successfully replaced minicomputers but these do not make up the bulk of their uses. The following properties generally typify most microprocessor applications.

a) The application must have some need for logical control. This may be either a time sequencing operation or a situation where the operations performed depend on the input data. If there are no decisions to be made, it is probably not a microprocessor application.

b) The application typically does not require significant numeric calculations. Although microprocessors can perform sophisticated arithmetic operations, they do so somewhat slowly. If significant computations are required, a minicomputer is usually the best course.

c) Although microprocessors can perform hundreds of thousands of operations each second, they are not as fast as well-designed parallel hardwired logic. The applications where their speed is not a problem are typically those which involve an interaction with humans. If the calculations or decisions must be made at speeds in the tens or hundreds of kilohertz, a microprocessor may not be the answer.

d) The cost of the microprocessor must be appropriate to the cost of the system. A very complex system will typically use a minicomputer since the overall cost difference is small and the minicomputer is typically easier to use.

e) A microprocessor is well suited to communicating with the outside world and many microprocessor applications have a great deal of input and output (I/O)

f) The use of a microprocessor can make a system extremely flexible. Thus, the same physical device can be called upon to perform different operations in different situations. By simply changing the program which drives the microprocessor, the overall functioning of the device can be changed.

There are a vast range of actual and potential applications

of microprocessors. You may be familiar with the Amana microwave oven which lets the housewife program a sequence of cooking steps. It uses a small microprocessor to control the timing and sequencing of the various cooking cycles. Similar uses are planned for microprocessors in other home appliances such as washing machines.

Many people in the electronics business are familiar with the increased use of microprocessors in test equipment. Automatic ranging digital volt meters and oscilloscopes are becoming more and more common. The microprocessors let the test equipment automatically adapt to changing use patterns and make it far more versatile.

Many manufacturers are now using microprocessors to control computer terminals. This permits the terminals to be more flexible in their response to human operators and the main computer. In addition, it lets the manufacturer sell numerous variations of the same piece of hardware without having to redesign his circuits. He simply modifies the program for the microprocessor and the device changes its characteristics.

Microprocessors have been proposed for use in numerous situations which use hardwired logic. For example, traffic light controllers currently require dozens of integrated circuits. If microprocessors were used, the number of packages required could be significantly reduced. Another similar application is the control of a bank of elevators. In both cases, the controller does a fair amount of input and output and only limited computation.

The advent of point-of-sale terminals has provided another large market for microprocessors. They allow the individual terminal to do some of the information processing such as adding tax and computing discounts before sending the information to a main computer. Another application in the retail area is automatic scales. These scales weigh an item and print a price tag containing the weight and the price. This function is currently performed by units using hardwired logic but the use of a microprocessor permits a significantly lower price for the scale.

The list of present and potential applications is virtually endless. In additon to the examples above, microprocessors have been proposed for use in electronic games, automatic gas pumps, process control, teaching aids, and so on.

The exciting thing about microprocessors is that the basic techniques used in all these applications are the same. The designer must first determine what hardware is required to provide the microprocessor with the inputs that it needs; he must decide what outputs are required; then he must write the program which allows the microprocessor to compute the outputs from the inputs. In this book, we will first examine the basic concepts of programming and then connect them with the hardware techniques required for input and output.

1.3 Outline of the Book

The next three chapters have been designed to acquaint the reader with the basic principles of stored program machines. They will describe how to enter a sequence of instructions and have the same hardware perform a number of different tasks. The concept of storing a program in memory and having the computer execute it will be illustrated. In addition to the programming concepts involved, the details of binary representations, hexadecimal numbers, and the hardware required to store programs will be explained. Chaper 5 is concerned with jump commands which permit the programmer to change the sequence in which instructions are executed, while Chapter 6 examines the methods of storing and retrieving data from memory.

Chapters 7 through 11 introduce various system programs and advanced programming concepts which facilitate the preparation of user programs. Chapter 7 discusses system utility software which gives the user the ability to analyze what the computer is doing. A detailed investigation of the use of teletype and teletype-like terminals is presented in Chapter 8. Chapters 9 and 10 are devoted to the advanced software techniques that are required for more sophisticated applications of microprocessors. Both editors and assemblers are introduced, and examples using them are presented. The concept of sub-routines is presented in Chapter 11.

The next four chapters, Chapter 12 through 15, are devoted primarily to an investigation of the hardware used in microcomputer systems. This includes details of the microprocessor itself as well as explanations of a number of interface devices and peripheral equipment. With this background in hardware, it is possible to discuss a number of system design projects which would involve microprocessors.

Chapter 16 compares some of the vast array of microprocessors currently available, and Chapter 17 discusses various other methods of program development.

BASIC MACHINE STRUCTURE

We begin the study of microprocessor systems by examining a very simple computer structure. Although this system can only do a limited number of things, it will allow us to introduce a number of important concepts without unnecessary complexity. The structure described in this chapter is only part of the 8080. We will add additional structure in later chapters.

2.1 Bits and Bytes

As with any digital computer system, all information in a microprocessor is represented as a sequence of *bits.* A bit is a single-element binary number whose value is either 0 or 1. A bit may, for example, represent the status of a switch as off or on or whether a door is open or closed.

The microprocessor that we will be studying, the 8080, is an *eight-bit* machine. That is, all information in the computer is actually in the form of sequences of eight bits. Each eight-bit sequence is referred to as a *word* or a *byte.* In general, a given byte can have as its value any one of the $2^8 = 256$ possible eight-bit sequences. For example, 10101101 could be the value of a byte as could 00111001.

2.2 System Structure

The simple microcomputer system structure that we will study in this section is shown in Fig. 2.1. The Central Processing Unit (CPU) is the heart of the system. Although what we have identified as the CPU, is more than just the microprocessor chip, it is convenient at this point to think of it as the microprocessor.

In addition to the CPU, Fig. 2.1 shows a set of eight

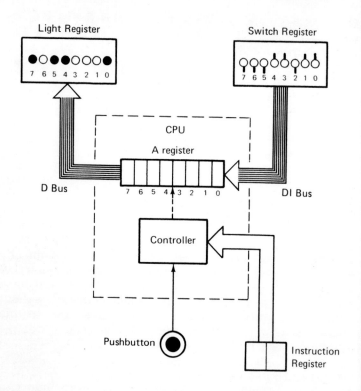

Figure 2.1 Basic microcomputer system structure.

switches which are connected to the CPU. The positions of these eight switches represent one byte of information and we will refer to it as the *Switch Register.* A set of eight lights is also shown as being connected to the CPU. Once again these eight lights represent one byte of information and will be referred to as the *Light Register.* The final items in Fig. 2.1 are a pushbutton and a box labeled *Instruction Register.* The Instruction Register contains a pair of *hexadecimal* thumbwheels; each thumbwheel can be set to any of the numbers from 0-9 or the letters A-F. These items will be used to tell the CPU what to do and we will discuss them later.

As we shall see, the bytes reside in various places within the microcomputer. One particularly important place is the *Accumulator.* The accumulator, or the A register, can be thought of as the heart of the computer. All information entering or leaving the computer must pass through it. Most arithmetic and logical operations involve the contents of this register. In the rest of this chapter, we shall see how to enter information into the A register; manipulate that information; and output the result of these manipulations.

It is important to note that each register always contains some eight-bit word; that is, it is never empty. If we think of the Light Register for a moment, we know that each of the eight lights is either on or off; there are no other possible states. In the same way, the A register always contains some eight-bit word.

There are two pathways, or *busses,* over which information can enter or leave the microcomputer. As shown in Fig. 2.1, these busses are *eight bits wide.* That is, every input or output instruction transfers eight bits, or one byte, into or out of the A register.

2.3 Instruction Concepts and Instruction Decoder

Operation of the computer is controlled by the sequence of instructions given to the control box, or *controller,* shown in Fig. 2.1. There are 244 possible instructions that this control box can execute. Initially, however, we will discuss only four of them. Each instruction has a name and a code. We will find it easier to refer to the instructions by name but the computer must be given its instructions by code. Each of these codes will consist of two symbols, each of which is either one of the numbers from 0 to 9 or one of the letters from A to F. Hence, possible instructions codes are 0A or AF or 93. We will see later why we choose this somewhat strange format for our instruction code.

We shall assume that our computer has been set up so that it will execute an instruction each time that the push-button is pushed. Later, we will see how to increase the speed at which the computer executes instructions by using an internal timing mechanism. However, at the beginning we want to make it go slowly and we assume that it is in the *single step* mode.

The first two instructions that we will discuss control the input and output busses. The first instruction is the INput instruction. The code for this instruction is DB. Its function is to transfer the information available on the input to the A register. However, as we shall see later, it is possible to have many different sources of this input data. Therefore, the INput instruction must be followed by a code which indicates from which of several possible input devices the information is to come. The codes for the input and output devices will have the same form as the instruction codes and can be assigned somewhat arbitrarily. We will use the code 02 to represent the input unit consisting of the eight switches.

Note that we have written the word input in the unusual fashion as INput above. It will be convenient for us to abreviate the instruction names. The abreviation for the input instruction is IN; to emphasis this we have written input in the form INput. We will follow this format as closely as possible throughout this book.

To load an eight-bit switch register word into the A register, one would first set up the eight switches to match the desired data pattern. Then the computer is given the INput instruction. To do this, the instruction DB is entered in the Instruction Register and the pushbutton is pushed. Then the code 02 is entered in the Instruction Register. Now, when the pushbutton is again pushed, the eight bit pattern in the Switch Register is transferred to the A register.

Note that the input operation takes two steps. First, the controller reads the code DB and decodes it as an INput operation. However, the input operation cannot be completed until the controller knows which input unit we want to use. Hence, the second step is to provide the code for the desired input unit, 02 in this case. Once this unit code is received, the controller carries out the input operation and transfers the eight bits represented by the switch positions into the A register.

The OUTput instruction, referred to as OUT, has the instruction code D3. Once again we may have several output devices and we must provide a unit code to tell the controller which unit we want to receive the output. We will assign the code 0B to the Light Register. To output the contents of the A register to the Light Register, the computer is first given the instruction code D3 and then code 0B. When this is done, the contents of the A register will be transferred to the lights. Once again, we see that this is a two step process: (1) the instruction code D3 is given and (2) the unit code 0B is given.

2.4 Sample Program
We can now write a very simple program to input or read data from the Switch Register and output it to the Light Register. First, however, we must decide on a convention for what is a one and what is a zero for each device. Let us make the up position of each switch be a one and the down position a zero. We will let a light indicate a one if it is off and a zero if it is on.

Consider the initial system status shown in Fig. 2.2 As we

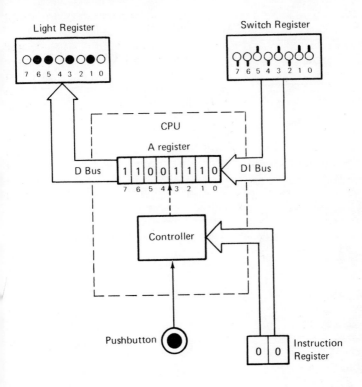

Figure 2.2 Initial status of system.

noted earlier, every register has something in it. In this case, the Switch Register represents the byte 00101011; the Light Register, 10010101; and the A register, 11001110. Note that they are all different. The Instruction Register shows the code 00. We could change the Switch Register to any other value without effecting the A or Light registers. The switches are only connected to the A register during the execution of an INput command.

Suppose that we wish to enter the byte 11110000 into the A register and then output it to the Light Register. We begin by setting switches 0 to 3 to the down position and 4 to 7 to the up position so that the Switch Register represents the byte 11110000.

The next step is to input this byte into the A register by the use of the INput command. Therefore we place the code DB into the Instruction Register and press the pushbutton. The system is now in the state shown in Fig. 2.3.

Note that the A and Light registers have not changed.

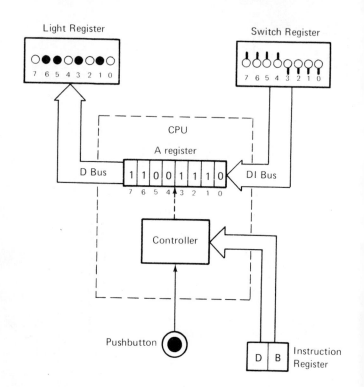

Figure 2.3   First step of input operation.

The INput command has not been completed because we must still provide the unit code for the desired input device. The next step is to place 02 in the Instruction Register and again press the pushbutton. The system now has the state shown in Fig. 2.4. Note that the data from the Switch Register has now been transfered to the A register. Once the pushbutton has been pressed, we could change the switches to any other positions without changing the A register.

To output the contents of the A register to the Light Register, we put the code D3 in the Instruction Register and press the pushbutton. Again Fig. 2.5 shows that no visible change occurs because the OUTput command has not been completed until the output unit code is given. Hence the next step is to place the code 0B into the Instruction Register and press the pushbutton again. Now the system has the status shown in Fig. 2.6 with lights 0 to 3 lit representing zeros and lights 4 to 7 off representing ones.

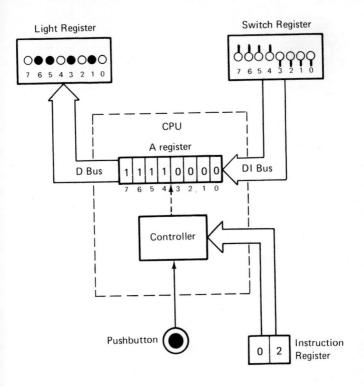

Figure 2.4 Second step of input operation.

We can summarize the program that we have just executed in the form shown in Table 2.1. Note that, even though we have written the input instruction on one line, we place the two codes, DB and 02, on separate lines to emphasize that they are separate steps. The program that we have just written is very simple and we could obviously accomplish the same goal of turning lights on with switches without the use of a microprocessor. However, the concepts involved in this simple example are powerful ones and will serve as the basis for much of what we do in the rest of this book.

TABLE 2.1 Simple Input/Output Program.

Code	Instruction Abbreviation	Comment
DB	IN 02	INPUT DATA
02		
D3	OUT 0B	OUTPUT
0B		

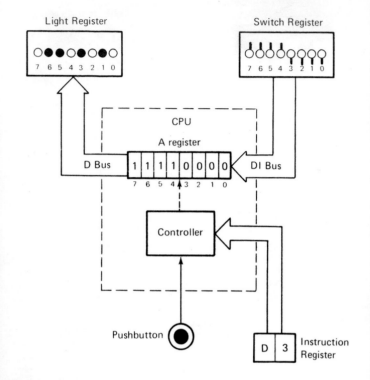

Figure 2.5   First step of output operation.

2.5 Rotate and Complement Instructions

Two additional instructions which permit some simple manipulations with the contents of the A register are the Rotate Right instruction, abbreviated RRC, and the CoMplement Accumulator instruction, abbreviated CMA. The RRC instruction replaces the zeroth bit of the A register with the first bit, the first with the second and so forth until the seventh bit is replaced by the original zeroth bit. This is shown diagrammatically in Fig. 2.7. This instruction makes the A register behave like a shift register with an end-around loop.

The CMA instruction changes the "polarity" of all of the eights bits in the A register. That is, if a bit were a 0, a CMA instruction will change it to a 1 and if a bit were a 1, CMA will change it to a 0. The code for the RRC instruction is 0F, while the code for CMA is 2F.

To illustrate the use of the RRC and CMA instructions, let us consider the operation of the program given in Table 2.2.

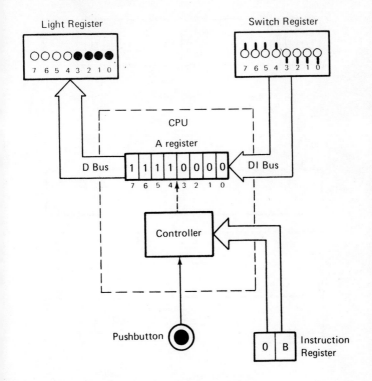

Figure 2.6 Second step of output operation.

This program inputs data from the Switch Register, rotates the byte one bit right, complements the A register, and then outputs the result to the Light Register.

TABLE 2.2 Program Using RRC and CMA Instructions.

Code	Instruction Abbreviation	Comment
DB	IN 02	INPUT DATA
02		
0F	RRC	ROTATE A REGISTER
2F	CMA	COMPLEMENT A
D3	OUT 0B	OUTPUT DATA
0B		

If we set the Switch Register to 11000111 and carry out the steps of this program, we find that the Light Register contains 00011100. The reader is urged to draw a set of dia-

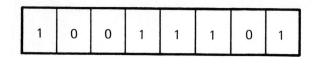

(a) A register before RRC instruction.

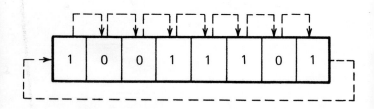

(b) Operation of RRC instruction.

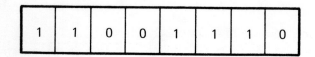

(c) A register after RRC instruction.

Figure 2.7   Operation of the RRC instruction.

grams similar to Figs. 2.2 to 2.6 to demonstrate the operation of this program and the state of the system after every step.

2.6 Exercises
For each of the exercises given below, the reader should draw a series of diagrams similar to Figs. 2.2 to 2.6 to show the state of the system after each step.
1) If the Switch Register is set to 11010111, find the contents of the Light Register after the program of Table 2.2 is executed.
2) Write a program which will input the contents of the Switch Register, rotate the A register twice and then output the result to the Light Register. What will be the contents of the Light Register if the Switch Register is set to 11110000 and this program is executed?

3

MORE MACHINE STRUCTURE

In this chapter we will add some more items to our machine structure and introduce some additional instructions. With these new tools, we will be able to solve more interesting problems.

3.1 Introduction of Additional Registers

In addition to the A register described in Chapter 2, there are several other registers available in the computer. At this time, we would like to introduce four more registers. These are referred to (conveniently) as the B register, the C register, the D register, and the E register. As with the A register, they represent places in the computer where eight-bit words can be stored. However, unlike the A register, it is not possible to do manipulations directly on these registers. For example, it is not possible to directly rotate the B register.

With the additional registers, the system structure is now as shown in Fig. 3.1. Note that the five registers are all interconnected, but that only the A register is connected to the input and output busses. All information must enter the system through the A register and all outputs must also use the A register.

3.2 MOVe Instructions

The principal use for these registers is to store information. As a result, the most frequently used instruction regarding the registers is the MOVe instruction. This instruction is used to move the information in one register to another register without changing the contents of the first register. As shown in Table 3.1, there are actually a large number of

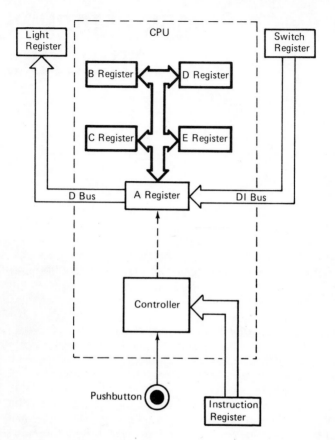

Figure 3.1   Additional registers.

MOVe instructions. For example, to MOVe the contents of the A register into the B register, we use MOV B,A. Note that the instruction format gives the destination, B in this case, followed by the origin of the information, A in this case. The MOVe instruction is easier to remember if we read it as "load". Hence, the instruction MOV E,A can be read as load E with A. As Table 3.1 shows, it is possible to MOVe the contents of any register to any other register.

If the Instruction Register is set at 4F and the pushbutton pressed, the contents of the A register will be copied into the C register. The A Register will *not* be affected! An important concept to remember is: whenever information is transferred from one place to another, the origin of the information is not changed. For example, when we transferred the contents of the A register to the Light Register, the

TABLE 3.1 MOVe Instructions.

Instruction	Code	Instruction	Code	Instruction	Code
MOV B, C	41	MOV C, A	4F	MOV E, D	5A
MOV B, D	42	MOV D, B	50	MOV E, A	5F
MOV B, E	43	MOV D, C	51	MOV A, B	78
MOV B, A	47	MOV D, E	53	MOV A, C	79
MOV C, B	48	MOV D, A	57	MOV A, D	7A
MOV C, D	4A	MOV E, B	58	MOV A, E	7B
MOV C, E	4B	MOV E, C	59		

contents of the A register remained unchanged.

To illustrate the use of these instructions, let us consider inputting two different bytes from the Switch Register and then outputting those bytes in the reverse order. It will be necessary to store the first byte somewhere before we input the second byte, otherwise the second byte would be written right over the first.

Let the initial byte in the Switch Register be 11001100. We carry out the usual input operation by placing the codes DB and 02 in the Instruction Register and pressing the pushbutton after each is entered. The resulting system status is shown in Figure 3.2. Note that all of the registers have something in them.

Now, to store this first byte, we use the instruction MOV B,A to place the contents of A into B. Hence, we set the code 47 and press the pushbutton. The system now has the state shown in Fig. 3.3. Note that the A register is un-

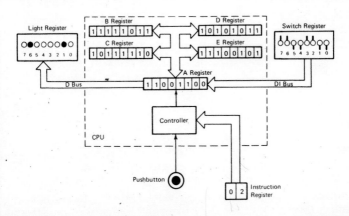

Figure 3.2 After first input.

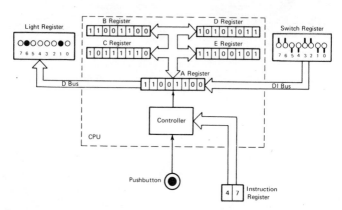

Figure 3.3 After storing A in B.

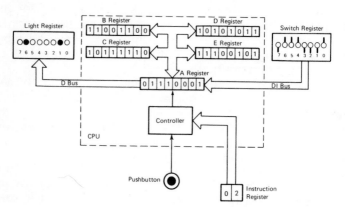

Figure 3.4 After second input.

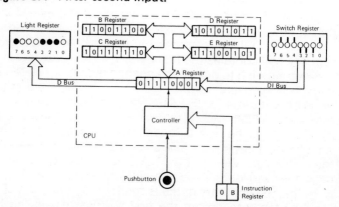

Figure 3.5 After first output.

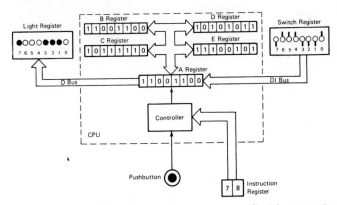

Figure 3.6 After MOVe operation to restore first byte to A.

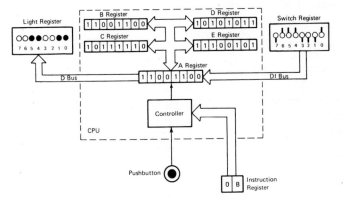

Figure 3.7 Final system state.

changed. The next step is to input the second byte. Set the
Switch Register to 01110001 and carry out the ususal input
procedure. The resulting system state is shown in Fig. 3.4.
Now the A register contains the second byte while the B
register still contains the first byte.

Since we wish to output the second byte first, we can just
carry out the usual output procedure. We set D3 and then
0B in the Instruction Register and press the pushbutton
after each. This result in the system state is shown in Fig.
3.5. To output the first byte we must retrieve it from the B
register and put it back in A since we can only output from
the A register. We use the MOV A,B instruction to accomplish this and obtain the system state shown in Fig. 3.6.
Note that the contents of the B register are unchanged. We
are now ready to output the first byte as usual. The final
system state is shown in Fig. 3.7. The Switch Register still

contains the second byte while the A, B and Light registers contain the first byte. The complete program for the above operation is summarized in Table 3.2.

TABLE 3.2   Program using MOVe Instructions.

Code	Instruction Abbreviation	Comment
DB 02	IN 02	INPUT FIRST BYTE
47	MOV B, A	STORE IN B
DB 02	IN 02	INPUT SECOND BYTE
D3 0B	OUT 0B	OUTPUT SECOND BYTE
78	MOV A, B	RESTORE FIRST BYTE
D3 0B	OUT 0B	OUTPUT FIRST BYTE

With the above example, we have demonstrated one of the powerful features of program control. We have made no hardware changes but have now been able to make our system execute a completely new task.

3.3 Logic Instructions

Although it is not possible to do logical and arithmetic operations on the contents of the B, C, D and E registers, it is possible to use the contents of these registers in pair-wise operations involving the A register. For example, it is possible to perform all of the basic logic operations: AND, OR and eXclusive OR (XOR) between the A Register and any of the other registers. The result will be stored in A and the other register will be unaffected. Each of these logical operations are carried out on a bit-by-bit basis. In effect, eight parallel logical operations are accomplished with one instruction.

For those not familiar with logical operations, an AND operation follows the same rules as bit by bit multiplication. Thus, for example, if the first bit in the A register and the first bit in the B register are both ones, the result of the AND operation would be a 1 in the first position. If either bit or both bits are 0's, the result of the AND operation would be a 0.

In a logical OR operation between A and B, the result is a

1 if either or both of the bits in the A or B registers are 1.
The eXclusive OR is similar to an OR operation except the
result is zero if both operands are 1. Hence the eXclusive
OR yields a 1 only if the operands are different and a 0 if
both are either 1 or 0. These logical operations are summarized in Table 3.3. The instruction abbreviations and codes
are summarized in Table 3.4.

TABLE 3.3 Description of Logical Operations.

(a) Logical AND: $c = a \cdot b$

	a = 0	a = 1
b = 0	c = 0	c = 0
b = 1	c = 0	c = 1

(b) Logical OR: $c = a + b$

	a = 0	a = 1
b = 0	c = 0	c = 1
b = 1	c = 1	c = 1

(c) Logical XOR: $c = a \oplus b$

	a = 0	a = 1
b = 0	c = 0	c = 1
b = 1	c = 1	c = 0

For example, if the A register contained the word
00001111 and the B register contained 10101010, then the
result of an AND carried out between A and B would be
00001010. The result of an OR operation on these same
registers would be 10101111 while the result of an XOR
operation would be 10100101. When carrying out an AND
operation, if there is a zero in a given bit position in one of
the registers then a zero will result in that position regardless of the other register. In the same way, during an OR
operation, if there is a 1 in a given bit position in one of the
registers, then the result will have a 1 in that position. On
the other hand, if there is a 1 in a given bit position and we
do an AND operation, then the result will match the bit in
the other register. This same result will occur for a 0 and the
OR operation.

TABLE 3.4   Logical Instructions.

AND Instruction	Codes	OR Instruction	Codes	XOR Instruction	Codes
ANA B	A0	ORA B	B0	XRA B	A8
ANA C	A1	ORA C	B1	XRA C	A9
ANA D	A2	ORA D	B2	XRA D	AA
ANA E	A3	ORA E	B3	XRA E	AB

The property described above can be very useful if we want only to consider some part of a byte of information. Suppose, for example, that we want to know the status of bits 0 and 1 in the A register but don't care what the other bits are. If the B register is 00000011 and we AND the A and B registers, then bits 2 through 7 of the A register will become zero while bits 0 and 1 will be unaffected. The bit pattern in B is referred to as a *mask* because it masks off some of the bits in A.

3.4 Exercises
Once again, for each of these exercises the reader should draw a set of system status diagrams like Figs. 3.2 to 3.7 to visualize the operation of the system.
1) Write a program which will read a sequence of three words from the Switch Register and then output them in the inverse order to the Light Register. That is, you should read a word, store it, read another word, store it, and then read a third word and store it. Then, you should display the third word in the lights, then the second word, then the first word.
2) The objective of this exercise is to read a word from the switch register and then output to the light register bits 1, 2 and 3 as set on the switches and zeros for all other positions independent of the switch settings. To do so, you will first read a "mask" from the Switch Register and store it in register B. You will then read an input word from the Switch Register, mask it by doing an AND operation and then output the result.

4 STORED PROGRAMS

In this chapter, we will learn what sets a computer apart from simply a complicated calculator. We will see how it is possible to write a program, store it in the computer's memory, and then have the computer execute this program. Before we do so, however, we will need to introduce the octal and hexadecimal representations of binary numbers.

4.1 Hexadecimal, Octal and Binary Numbers

Consider for a moment a three-bit binary number. There are only eight possible values of a three-bit number and they are listed in Table 4.1. If you are familiar with binary arithmetic, you will note that the column on the left is the result of adding a 1 to the preceding number in binary arithmetic. Thus, it is actually a numerical sequence. The column on the right is the sequence of numbers from 0 to 7. Each entry is the value of the corresponding binary number. Since there are eight possible numbers, we say that this column is the *octal* representation of the number.

TABLE 4.1 Binary-to-Octal Conversion.

Binary	Octal
000	0
001	1
010	2
011	3
100	4
101	5
110	6
111	7

There is an easy way to remember this table. If we let the three bits of the binary number be a_2, a_1 and a_0, then the octal number is equal to $4(a_2) + 2(a_1) + a_0$. For example, the binary number 011 has $a_2 = 0$, $a_1 = 1$ and $a_0 = 1$ so that the octal equivalent is $4(0) + 2(1) + 1 = 3$, as shown in the table.

As noted at the outset, the computer we are using has 8-bit words. The system described above for enumerating three-bit sequences can be generalized for the eight-bit case. Consider dividing the eight bits of a word into three pieces as shown below:

xx xxx xxx

The right-most three bits can obviously be represented by an octal number between 0 and 7. Similarly, the next set of three bits can also be represented by a number between 0 and 7. Finally, the left-most two bits can be represented by an integer between 0 and 3. Therefore, any eight-bit binary number can be represented as a three-digit number between 000 and 377. Note, however, that none of these three-digit numbers contain the digits 8 or 9 in any position. These three-digit numbers are actually *octal* numbers. Whenever confusion might arise, we will use a subscript 8 at the end of the number to indicate that it is an octal, rather than an ordinary base 10 number. For example, the octal number 123 would be written as 123_8. Note that, if the number contains any 8s or 9s, it cannot be octal.

There is another representation of eight-bit binary numbers which is also very useful. In this case, we divide the number into two four-bit groups. A four-bit number has $2^4 = 16$ different possible values. Because we have only ten ordinary single numerals (0,1,2,...,9), we must add six new symbols. The first six letters of the alphabet have been selected for this purpose. This numbering system is known as *hexadecimal*. The binary-to-hexadecimal conversion is summarized in Table 4.2.

We propose to divide the eight-bit binary number into two four-bit binary numbers in the form

xxxx xxxx

Each of the four-bit groups can be written as one of the sixteen hexadecimal characters. Hence the eight-bit binary word (byte) becomes a two-character hexadecimal number between 00 and FF. This format is somewhat more convenient than the octal representation, since we need only two characters rather than three and it will be the one

TABLE 4.2 Binary-to-Hexadecimal Conversion.

Binary	Hexadecimal	Binary	Hexadecimal
0000	0	1000	8
0001	1	1001	9
0010	2	1010	A
0011	3	1011	B
0100	4	1100	C
0101	5	1101	D
0110	6	1110	E
0111	7	1111	F

that we will primarily use. When we want to specifically label a number as hexadecimal, we will use an "H" subscript or suffix at the end. Of course, any number with the letters A to F in it must be hexadecimal. Table 4.3. provides an easy method for converting between octal and hexadecimal.

4.2 Immediate Instructions

You will note by looking at the two previous chapters that all instruction codes are actually two-character hexadecimal numbers. The computer translates the hexadecimal numbers residing in the Instruction Register into eight-bit binary numbers which it uses internally.

With this hexadecimal-to-binary conversion procedure in mind, it is possible to introduce the *immediate* instructions. These instructions enable a programmer to enter information directly into the registers. For example, the instruction MVI A (MoVe Immediate A register) causes the computer to read the next instruction code, convert it to a binary number, and place it in the accumulator. There are MoVe Immediate instructions for all registers as shown in Table 4.4. To load the B register with the byte A6 (i.e. 10100110), we would first place the code 06 in the Instruction Register and press the pushbutton. Next, we would put A6 in the Instruction Register and again press the pushbutton. The abbreviation that we would use for this operation is MVI B,A6.

If you are beginning to have trouble remembering all of the instructions and their codes, you may wish to begin to refer to Appendices A and B at the end of the book. Appendix A contains a listing of all of the 8080 instructions arranged alphabetically by instruction abbreviation and gives the detailed description of each instruction. Appendix

TABLE 4.3 Octal to Hexadecimal Conversion.

Least Significant Character

	0	1	2	3	4	5	6	7	8	9	A	B	C	D	E	F
0	000	001	002	003	004	005	006	007	010	011	012	013	014	015	016	017
1	020	021	022	023	024	025	026	027	030	031	032	033	034	035	036	037
2	040	041	042	043	044	045	046	047	050	051	052	053	054	055	056	057
3	060	061	062	063	064	065	066	067	070	071	072	073	074	075	076	077
4	100	101	102	103	104	105	106	107	110	111	112	113	114	115	116	117
5	120	121	122	123	124	125	126	127	130	131	132	133	134	135	136	137
6	140	141	142	143	144	145	146	147	150	151	152	153	154	155	156	157
7	160	161	162	163	164	165	166	167	170	171	172	173	174	175	176	177
8	200	201	202	203	204	205	206	207	210	211	212	213	214	215	216	217
9	220	221	222	223	224	225	226	227	230	231	232	233	234	235	236	237
A	240	241	242	243	244	245	246	247	250	251	252	253	254	255	256	257
B	260	261	262	263	264	265	266	267	270	271	272	273	274	275	276	277
C	300	301	302	303	304	305	306	307	310	311	312	313	314	315	316	317
D	320	321	322	323	324	325	326	327	330	331	332	333	334	335	336	337
E	340	341	342	343	344	345	346	347	350	351	352	353	354	355	356	357
F	360	361	362	363	364	365	366	367	370	371	372	373	374	375	376	377

Most Significant Character

TABLE 4.4   MoVe Immediate Instructions.

Abbreviation	Code
MVI A	3E
MVI B	06
MVI C	0E
MVI D	16
MVI E	1E

B has the instructions arranged in functional groups. We will not discuss all of the 8080 instructions in the text of this book so that Appendix A will serve as an introduction to those instructions not covered. The back cover of this book is a table of instructions cross-referenced by hexadecimal code.

4.3 Use of Memory for Program Storage

We are now ready to begin the discussion of storing a program in memory before it is executed. To do so, we must first discuss what memory is available to us in the computer. As with the registers, the memory is a set of places where eight-bit binary numbers can be stored. There are, however, far more memory locations than there are registers. For now, we will be permitted to use only 256 different memory locations. Later we will see that this is only one *page* of memory and that there can be many pages.

With so many different locations, it is clearly easier to refer to them by number rather than by name. Therfore, they are numbered consecutively starting at zero. However, since the computer must also use these numbers, they are given in hexadecimal rather than decimal. Thus, the location numbers are: 00, 01, 02, 03, 04, 05, 06, 07, 08, 09, 0A, 0B, ..., FE, FF.

To understand how the program executes instructions from memory, we must enlarge our drawing of the computer system itself. In Fig. 4.1, we have added both the *program memory* and the device labeled *program counter*. The program counter is a binary register which stores the address of the next instruction. Therefore, when you begin to execute your program, the program counter is automatically set to 0. After retrieving an instruction, it is "incremented". That is, its contents are increased by 1. Therefore, the computer will be ready to read the instruction stored in the next word. In this way, the computer sequentially reads the content of memory just as it sequen-

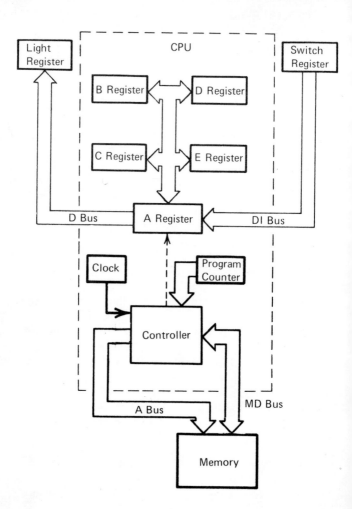

Figure 4.1 Memory for program storage.

tially read the content of the Instruction Register earlier.

When we were entering instructions manually, we told the computer when to execute the next instruction by pushing a pushbutton. When the computer is operating in its normal mode, however, there is no time to press a pushbutton. Rather, there is a clock inside the computer which fulfills the function of the pushbutton. Every 2.5 microseconds or so, this clock tells the computer to read the next instruction. This allows the computer to execute instructions very rapidly. When the internal clock calls for the next instruction, the CPU sends the address from the program counter out to memory on the A bus. The memory responds by placing the contents of this location on the MD bus. The CPU then reads this data and proceeds to the next step.

4.4 Entering Programs into Memory

Every computer system has some method for entering instructions into memory. We will describe one of the more common approaches; various possible modifications will also be noted. The system is shown schematically in Fig. 4.2. The system has three eight-bit registers, two pushbuttons, and one toggle switch as shown. The Memory Location Register, which can be a set of eight switches or two hexadecimal thumbwheels, will be used to set the address of the memory location which we wish to display or alter. The Memory Contents Register, which can be eight lights or two hexadecimal digit displays, will display the contents of memory specified by the Memory Location Register. Finally

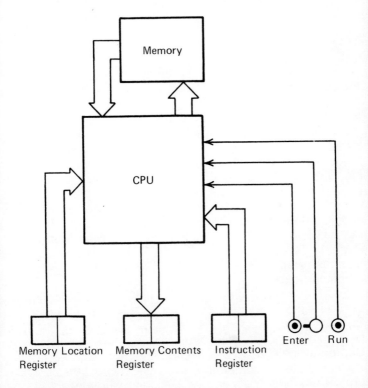

Figure 4.2 Program entry system.

the Instruction Register will be used for setting the instruction code that we wish to store in a given memory location. Although each of these registers may be in hexadecimal or binary form, we will assume that they are hexadecimal.

Before entering a program into memory, it is highly desirable to write out both the instruction codes and the abbreviations. We also need to add the memory locations for each instruction. A simple program, written in this format, is given in Table 4.5. The program reads a byte from the Switch Register, complements it and then outputs it to the Light Register.

TABLE 4.5 A Simple Program.

Location	Code	Instruction
00	DB	IN 02
01	02	
02	2F	CMA
03	D3	OUT 0B
04	0B	

Once you have finished writing the program, you are ready to load it into the computer. To begin, your first word of program should be stored in location 00. The toggle switch should be to the left so that the computer is ready to store instructions in memory. Place the code of the first instruction of your program in the Instruction Register as before. Then set the Memory Location Register to the location where you wish to store this instruction. For your first instruction, this will be location 00. When you have completed this, depress the pushbutton labeled ENTER, and your instruction will be stored in location 00. To store the next word of your program, place it in the Instruction Register, set the Memory Location Register to 01 and depress the ENTER button. Continue this process until all of the program has been entered.

The Memory Contents Register will display the contents of the memory location specified by the Memory Location Register. When we first set the Memory Location Register to 00, some unspecified byte will appear in the Memory Contents Register. This is because memory locations must always contain something. However, after the ENTER button has been pushed, the DB code will appear. In this way, it is possible to check that each instruction has been correctly entered. After you are satisfied that you have correctly entered your program, you should enter any input data in the Switch Register, then run the program by putting the toggle switch to the right and depressing the RUN pushbutton. You will notice that your program runs extremely quickly. In fact, it seems to take no time at all. Actually, it probably took somewhere around 0.1 millisecond.

If you wish to run your program again, you may do so by pushing the run button again. Therefore, you can run the same program on a large set of data without having to reenter the program each time new data is used.

4.5 Types of Memory

Since we have begun to use memory, this is a good time to note the two different types of memory which are used in microcomputers. The memory in which your program was stored is referred as *Random Access Memory* (RAM). This name was originated to differentiate this type of memory from magnetic tape where the computer must access memory in a sequential fashion. Currently, however, it is used to indicate memory which the computer may both write into and also read from. When you entered your instructions, the computer wrote them into memory. When you pushed the RUN button, the computer went back and read what it had written. In the microcomputers we are discussing, this memory is contained in small integrated circuits each capable of remembering 1024 bits. Other chips are available that can store up to 4096 or 16,384 bits.

The other type of memory used in microcomputers is referred to as *Read Only Memory* (ROM). This is a type of memory which the computers, in normal operation, can read from but cannot write into. Thus, for example, certain *systems* programs which are used to control the computer are written into these Read Only Memories by a special process. There are several types of Read Only Memories. Those referred to as ROM's have their contents built into them when the integrated circuit is built. A more complete name for this type of device is *metal-mask ROM.* This name results from the use of a mask in the process of building the device.

Another type of Read Only Memory is referred to as the PROM. This stands for Programmable Read Only Memory. These devices are manufactured with *blank* memories and the memory content is *burned in* by the user. A special device is used and voltages well above the operating range are required to alter the contents of the PROM. This "burning in" can be done either by the user or by a service organization.

A final variation of Read Only Memories are EPROM's. These are Erasable Programmable Read Only Memories. They differ from PROM's only in that it is possible to erase their contents. This is done by exposing them to ultraviolet light for a considerable period of time.

4.6 Arithmetic Instructions

The 8080 is capable of doing simple addition and subtraction on eight-bit binary numbers. Basically, it does binary arithmetic; when it adds two binary numbers together, the result is a binary number which is the binary representation of the sum of the two original numbers. For example, if A contains the binary representation of 19 (00010011) and B contains the binary representation of 6 (00000110), then the result of adding them will be the binary representation of 25 (00011001). The 8080 computes this by doing binary addition according to the rules:

$$0 + 0 = 0$$
$$1 + 0 = 1$$
$$1 + 1 = 0, \text{carry } 1$$

Thus, to add 25 and 6, the 8080 computes

```
    00010011
  + 00000110
    00011001
```

In a similar way, the 8080 can subtract numbers using binary subtraction. For example, to subtract 6 from 19, the 8080 does

```
    00010011
  - 00000110
    00001101
```

and gets the binary representation for 13.

If only positive numbers were to be used, the 8080 could represent all of the integers in the range 0 to 255. However, it is usually desirable to permit negative numbers also. Therefore, only numbers in the range –128 to 127 are available directly. Wider ranges of numbers can be accommodated using sophisticated techniques.

A special convention, called *two's complement notation*, is used by almost all microprocessors, including the 8080, to represent negative numbers. At first it will probably sound quite arbitrary and confusing but we will show that it is actually very well thought out. To find the binary representation of a negative number, –N, there are two steps:

> a) Complement all of the bits in
>   the representation of N.
> b) Add 00000001 .

Thus, for example, to find the binary representation of –19, one takes the representation of 19 given by 00010011, complements it to obtain 11101100 and then adds one to yield 11101101.

To show that this process is sensible, one must be able to negate a negative number and get back the original positive value. If we try this with –19, we take the binary representation which is 11101101, complement it as 00010010 and then add one to obtain 00010011 which is 19!

Note that if we only allow positive numbers up to 127, the leftmost bit will always be 0. Similarly, if we do not permit negative numbers lower than –128, the leftmost bit will always be 1. Thus, this bit actually represents the sign of the number, 1 for negative and 0 for positive.

To show that this procedure is very useful, consider subtracting 19 from 0. Using standard binary subtraction, we have

$$
\begin{array}{r}
00000000 \\
- \ \underline{00010011} \\
11101101
\end{array}
$$

which is exactly –19. Note that we have assumed that we can borrow one from a fictional ninth bit to the left of the eight-bit representation of zero.

Another nice feature is that if standard binary addition is performed between a negative and a positive number or two negative numbers, the correct result is found. For example, adding –19 to 25 yields

$$
\begin{array}{r}
00011001 \\
+ \ \underline{11101101} \\
00000110
\end{array}
$$

which is 6! If you work this example through, you will note that there is a carry bit from the eighth position that is ignored.

Adding two negative numbers also works. Consider adding –14 and –36. First, we must find the appropriate two's complement notation. For –14, we take the representation for 14 which is 00001110, complement it to obtain 11110001, and then add one to give 11110010.

In a similar fashion, we find that –36 is 11011100. We then perform the addition

$$
\begin{array}{r}
11110010 \\
+ \ \underline{11011100} \\
11001110
\end{array}
$$

Since the leftmost bit is a one, this is clearly a negative number. To evaluate it, we will find the corresponding positive number by complementing it to obtain 00110001 and then adding one to yield 00110010. The result is the representation of $32 + 16 + 2 = 50$ as expected.

Some of the arithmetic instructions available on the 8080 are summarized in Table 4.6. These instructions all operate between the indicated register and the A register and leave the result in A. For example, ADD B adds the contents of B to the contents of A and leaves the result in A. SUB D subtracts D from A and leaves the result in A.

TABLE 4.6   Arithmetic Instructions.

ADD		SUBtract	
Instruction	Codes	Instruction	Codes
ADD B	80	SUB B	90
ADD C	81	SUB C	91
ADD D	82	SUB D	92
ADD E	83	SUB E	93

4.7 Exercises

Each of these exercises specifies a simple program to be written. These programs should be written in the form of Table 4.5. If you have a microcomputer system available, load the programs into memory and see if they run.

1) Write a program that will turn on all of the lights in the Light Register independent of the Switch Register setting. How would you change this program to turn off all of the lights?

2) Write a program that will read the Switch Register, rotate it to the right twice, complement it and then display the result in the Light Register.

3) If you wish to try something more difficult, have the computer read the Switch Register and display in the lights a binary number equal to the number of ones in the switch register. This program requires some careful thought. It can, however, be done with only the instructions that we have discussed so far.

5 JUMP INSTRUCTIONS

So far we have considered programs which run only once and in a strictly sequential fashion. This is very restrictive! JuMP instructions allow us to alter the logical flow of a program and to cause conditional branching. The JuMP instructions accomplish this by providing a method of changing the Program Counter. Recall that the Program Counter tells the computer where to get the next instruction.

The use of JuMP instructions will significantly expand our programming possibilities. Before we can examine JuMP instructions, however, it is necessary to understand the memory structure of the 8080.

5.1 The Page Structure of Memory
The memory of the 8080 is organized into *pages* and *words.* There are 256 pages and each page has 256 words. To define a specific spot in memory, we must give both a page number *and* a word number. Hence one speaks of a location in memory such as "page 10, word D3." We will always use hexadecimal numbers when giving memory locations. We can write the above memory location in shorthand form as 10D3. Since 16 bits are required to specify a memory location, the A Bus of Fig. 4.1 is actually 16 bits wide. The analogy to pages and words in a book is helpful in visualizing the meaning of a memory location. Thus, 10D3 is word number $D3_H$ on page number 10_H.

5.2 Unconditional Jumps
The instruction JMP PPWW (where PP and WW denote two hexadecimal numbers) causes an unconditional jump to the location page PP and word WW. This JuMP is accomplished

by setting the program counter equal to PPWW. This instruction appears in memory as

```
C3
WW
PP
```

The C3 code tells the instruction decoder that this is the unconditional jump instruction and that the next two bytes of the instruction contain the address for the next instruction to be executed. Note that the page number is the *third* byte in this three-byte instruction.

With the use of the JMP instruction, we can write a program that will run repetitively or *loop*. Suppose, for example, that a program begins at location 0100. If we add the following instruction to the end of this program

```
C3    JMP 0100
00
01
```

then the program will run repetitively without stopping.

The program shown in Table 5.1 inputs the number set in the switches, lights the appropriate lights, and then repeats. The CMA instruction was added so that a switch up would correspond to a light on.

TABLE 5.1 Simple Looping Program.

Location	Code	Instruction	Comment
0100	DB	INP 02	INPUT
0101	02		
0102	2F	CMA	COMPLEMENT
0103	D3	OUT 0B	OUTPUT
0104	0B		
0105	C3	JMP 0100	JUMP TO START
0106	00		
0107	01		

5.3 Conditional Jumps

A conditional jump is one which occurs only if a certain condition is met. These instructions allow us to alter the logical flow of a program based on inputs received or on computed variables. This capability is the heart of a stored program controller. The instruction JZ PPWW causes a jump to the location PPWW if the *zero flag* is set (i.e., equal to 1). The code for this instruction is CA.

The zero flag is one bit of an eight-bit *Flag Register.* It can be set in two ways:

) With the execution of a logical or arithmetic operation that yields a zero result.

') With the execution of a *compare* instruction on two identical items.

here are two forms of compare instructions:

a) CoMPare the A register with another register. For example, to compare A with B, the instruction is CMP B. This instruction has the code B8. (The other CoMPare instructions are: CMP C = B9, CMP D = BA, CMP E = BB.)

b) There is also a ComPare Immediate instruction: CPI xx. This two byte instruction has the code

> FE
> xx

and it compares A with the hexadecimal coded byte xx.

Note: All compare instructions affect *only* the zero flag. The registers themselves are not changed.

5.4 Input Directed Programs

To carry out some of the programming tasks which we wish to consider in our later development, it is necessary to have an additional input unit. We have selected a pair of hexadecimal thumbwheels; these thumbwheels will generate one byte of information and we have assigned them the device code 03.

Our system now takes the form shown in Fig. 5.1 where the input/output device codes have been added to facilitate remembering them. We will describe how these thumbwheels are connected to the system in Chapter 13.

Let us repeat the program of Table 5.1 but have the program turn off all of the lights if the thumbwheels are set to 00. For any other thumbwheel setting, the Switch Register is inputted, complemented and outputted to the Light Register as before. The program, shown in Table 5.2, begins by reading the thumbwheels using the instruction IN 03. The value received from the thumbwheels is compared to zero. If the thumbwheels are zero, the program jumps to location 010F and turns off all of the lights by loading the A Register with all ones and then outputting it to the Light Register. If the thumbwheels are not 00, the program continues as before.

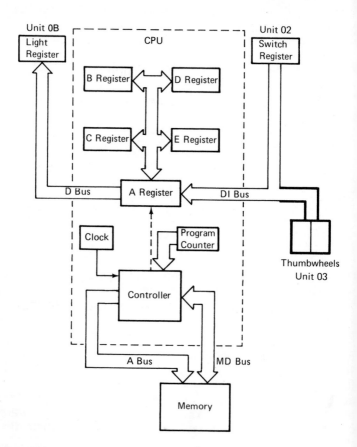

Figure 5.1 Addition of thumbwheel input.

5.5 Exercises

1) The objective of this exercise is to write a program to check your knowledge of hexadecimal and binary numbers. The program should operate in the following manner:

   a) An hexadecimal number is set in the thumbwheel switches.

   b) A binary number is set in the toggle switches.

   c) If the two numbers match, the computer lights the appropriate lights.

   d) If the two numbers do not match, no lights are lit.

   e) The program should run in a repetitive manner.

TABLE 5.2 Input Directed Program.

Location	Code	Instruction	Comment
0100	DB	IN 03	INPUT THUMBWHEELS
0101	03		
0102	FE	CPI 00	COMPARE TO ZERO
0103	00		
0104	CA	JZ 010F	JUMP IF ZERO
0105	0F		
0106	01		
0107	DB	IN 02	INPUT SWITCH REGISTER
0108	02		
0109	2F	CMA	COMPLEMENT
010A	D3	OUT 0B	OUTPUT TO LIGHT REGISTER
010B	0B		
010C	C3	JMP 0100	JUMP TO BEGINNING
010D	00		
010E	01		
010F	3E	MVI A, FF	TURN OFF LIGHTS
0110	FF		
0111	D3	OUT 0B	OUTPUT TO LIGHT REGISTER
0112	0B		
0113	C3	JMP 0100	JUMP TO BEGINNING
0114	00		
0115	01		

USE OF MEMORY FOR DATA STORAGE

So far we have talked about using memory only for program storage. Memory can also be used for data storage. In fact, it can function like another register. Figure 6.1 shows the MD bus extended to the register bank. The same bus is used to carry both instructions and data.

In order to use memory for data storage, we must have instructions for storing data in memory at the desired location and for retrieving it when needed. There are two general classes of instructions for data storage and retrieval:
1) Direct Addressing: Three-byte instructions which specify the memory location address to be used in bytes two and three (like a JMP instruction).
2) Register-indirect Addressing: One-byte instructions which use the HL register pair to provide the address.

6.1 Direct Addressing
There are two instructions in this class:

(a) LDA PPWW	3A	
	WW	
	PP	
(b) STA PPWW	32	
	WW	
	PP	

Note again that the *third* byte of the instruction contains the page number and the second byte contains the word number.

The LDA instruction LoaDs the A register with the *contents* of the memory location PPWW. Suppose that the first six words of page 4 are:

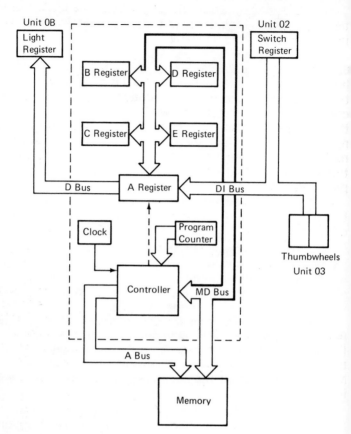

Figure 6.1   Memory for data storage.

Memory Location	Contents
0400	5A
0401	B9
0402	65
0403	4F
0404	B6
0405	FC

The execution of the instruction LDA 0403 would cause the A register to be loaded with 4F, while LDA 0400 would cause it to be loaded with 5A. In each case, the contents of the memory location is unchanged. Note that A is loaded with the contents of the specified memory location *not* with the address.

The "STA" instruction is the opposite of the LDA instruction. It causes the contents of the A register to be STored in the memory location PPWW.

6.2 Use of HL Register Pair

It is also possible to treat memory as if it were another register. In this case, the memory location is specified by the contents of two registers that we have not yet talked about, the HL register pair. Both H and L are standard eight-bit registers but together they form a sixteen-bit address register. The H register contains the high or page part of the address, while the L register contains the low or word part of the address.

If we wished to address the memory location 0C63 using this method, then we must set H = 0C and L = 63. This can be accomplished by executing the following code:

```
26      MVI  H,0C
0C
2E      MVI  L,63
63
```

Once the memory address has been placed in the HL register pair, it is possible to use that memory location as if it were another register. In particular, it is possible to move the contents of that memory location to any register by MOVe instructions. The hexadecimal codes for these instructions are:

MOV A,M	7E	MOV E,M	5E
MOV B,M	46	MOV H,M	66
MOV C,M	4E	MOV L,M	6E

Note that the instruction MOV A,M is functionally equivalent to LDA except that the address is in the HL registers for the MOV A,M instruction rather than in bytes two and three as in the LDA instruction.

It is also possible to transfer the contents of any register to memory by means of MOVe instructions. The hexadecimal codes for these instructions are:

MOV M,A	77	MOV M,E	73
MOV M,B	70	MOV M,H	74
MOV M,C	71	MOV M,L	75
MOV M,D	72		

The instruction MOV M,A is functionally equivalent to STA except, again, for the method of memory addressing.

There is also a MoVe Immediate instruction for memory,

MVI M, with the hexadecimal code 36. This two-byte instruction loads the memory location specified by HL with the contents of the second byte of the instruction. If we want to load 7D into location 0842, we could use the code:

```
26      MVI  H,08
08
2E      MVI  L,42
42
36      MVI  M,7D
7D
```

One might ask why we need these instructions using the HL register pair when it appears that we can do all of the same things with the LDA and STA instructions. For one thing, the HL memory instructions add flexibility and can lead to considerably shorter code in many cases. Since each byte in memory costs us something, shorter code means less expensive systems. Consider, for example, the problem of loading the B register with the contents of memory location 0752 when the A register has a result that we cannot destroy. The use of the LDA and STA would yield the following code:

```
4F      MOV  C,A        SAVE A IN C
3A      LDA  0752
52
07
47      MOV  B,A
79      MOV  A,C        RESTORE A
```

A functionally equivalent code using H and L is

```
26      MVI  H,07
07
2E      MVI  L,52
52
46      MOV  B,M
```

Here we have used five bytes versus six in the previous case.

The use of the HL register pair is particularly beneficial if we repeatedly need to address the same memory location or if we wish to address several locations in sequence. It is often desirable to store words into memory sequentially. To do this we can make use of the INcRement L instruction,

INR L (2C). This instruction adds one to the L register. If L = 377, the INR L instruction will add one, causing L to become all zeros, and the zero flag will be set to one. If L is not 377, the zero flag is set to zero.

Suppose that we want to load the first five words on page 06 with the contents of the A, B, C, D and E Registers. One possible code for this is

```
26      MVI   H,06
06
2E      MVI   L,00
00
77      MOV   M,A
2C      INR   L
70      MOV   M,B
2C      INR   L
71      MOV   M,C
2C      INR   L
72      MOV   M,D
2C      INR   L
73      MOV   M,E
```

As an exercise, write out a functionally equivalent code using the STA instruction and compare the number of bytes used.

6.3 Example of the Use of Memory
In the following example, memory will be used to store both data and the program. Actually, two related problems will be solved. In the first solution, the LDA instruction will be used and in the second, the HL register pair will be used.

The objective of the example is to write a program that will read the switches and compare them to a "password" stored in memory. If they match, all the lights will be turned on. If they don't, all the lights will be turned off. We will store the password in word 40 of page 01.

The program will first read the Switch Register and then store its contents in register B. It will then load the password into A from its memory location and compare the two. If they match, it will jump to a section of code that will output 00 (turn the lights on). If they don't match, it will output FF (turn them off). In both cases, it will jump back to the beginning of the program when it is finished. The program is as follows:

Location	Code	Instruction	Comment
0100	DB	IN 02	INPUT SWITCHES
0101	02		
0102	47	MOV B, A	STORE IN B
0103	3A	LDA 0140	LOAD PASSWORD
0104	40		
0105	01		
0106	B8	CMP B	COMPARE
0107	CA	JZ 0111	JUMP IF MATCH
0108	11		
0109	01		
010A	3E	MVI A, FF	
010B	FF		
010C	D3	OUT 0B	TURN OFF LIGHTS
010D	0B		
010E	C3	JMP 0100	LOOP BACK
010F	00		
0110	01		
0111	3E	MVI A, 00	
0112	00		
0113	D3	OUT 0B	TURN ON LIGHTS
0114	0B		
0115	C3	JMP 0100	LOOP BACK
0116	00		
0117	01		

A more complex version of this program would have a number of customers each with their own passwords. This expanded problem is an ideal one for application of the HL register pair method of addressing memory. Each password would be stored in a different memory location and the computer will use the customer's number to locate the appropriate password.

For convenience, we will assume that the customers are numbered 40, 41, 42, etc. and that they enter their number in the thumbwheels. The program must read the customer number, read the Switch Register, compare the switches to the password and properly set the lights.

The password for customer 40 will be assumed already to be stored in word 40 of page 01. For customer 41, the password will be in 0141 and so on. Therefore, to locate the password, the program will load H with 01 and load L with the customer number. The program is as follows:

Location	Code	Instruction	Comment
0100	26	MVI H, 01	LOAD PAGE NUMBER
0101	01		
0102	DB	IN 03	GET CUSTOMER NO.
0103	03		
0104	6F	MOV L, A	PUT IT INTO L
0105	DB	IN 02	INPUT SWITCHES
0106	02		
0107	BE	CMP M	COMPARE WITH PASSWORD
0108	CA	JZ 0112	JUMP IF MATCH
0109	12		
010A	01		
010B	3E	MVI A, FF	
010C	FF		
010D	D3	OUT 0B	TURN OFF LIGHTS
010E	0B		
010F	C3	JMP 0100	LOOP BACK
0110	00		
0111	01		
0112	3E	MVI A, 00	
0113	00		
0114	D3	OUT 0B	TURN ON LIGHTS
0115	0B		
0116	C3	JMP 0100	LOOP BACK
0117	00		
0118	01		

Both of these programs can be shortened by seven words if a SUBtract command is used in place of the CoMPare. Can you see how?

6.4 Exercises

1) The objective is to write a program which begins at memory location 0100. The purpose of this program is to display the contents of page 01 of memory. The particular memory location to be displayed will be set in the thumbwheel (Unit 03) and the contents should be displayed in the Light Register.
2) Write a program using the STA instruction which will store the A, B, C, D, and E registers into the first five words of page 06.

7 SYSTEM MONITORS

It has probably occurred to you by now, that entering instructions into the computer manually is a laborious and time consuming process. You have probably also guessed that there must be a better way; you are right, there is! It is possible to use a typewriter-like device to simplify the job of controlling the computer. To do so, the computer must have a special program, called a *system monitor,* stored in it. This chapter describes the features of a system monitor and shows you how to use one to simplify loading and running programs.

Before we begin to discuss system monitors, however, we must make a few comments regarding that typewriter-like device called a terminal. The most common terminal device is probably a model 33 Teletype. This device resembles an electric typewriter; it has an electromechanical keyboard and a mechanical printer. Many computer systems use CRT terminals instead of teletypes. These terminals have an electronic keyboard and a TV-like display tube. The least expensive computer systems generally use a standard television set in place of the CRT display.

The things that system monitors can do vary greatly depending on which computer you are using. Our objective in this chapter is only to analyze the use of a system monitor to enter and run programs. After you understand these elements, you should be able to figure out for yourself the other features of your system monitor.

7.1 Starting the Monitor
Most system monitors are loaded in Read Only Memory. Therefore, the computer can read the monitor but cannot change it during normal operations. The program is always

present in memory, even when the computer is turned off. In order to start the system monitor, all we need to do is to get the program running. There will be a beginning address for the monitor program and we must make the computer do a JMP to this location.

There are three ways of achieving this. Most microcomputers have a special push-button which forces the computer to do a jump to location 0000. Therefore, if the system monitor starts at location 0000, all we need do to get it running is to push this *reset* button.

Unfortunately, however, there are many good reasons not to start the system monitor at the location 0000. Therefore, pushing the reset button may not start the system monitor. It may be possible, however, to use the methods described in previous chapters to load a JMP to the beginning address of the system monitor in words 0000, 0001 and 0002. Then, pushing the reset button will force the computer to execute a jump to the first address of the system monitor.

Some microcomputers will execute single instructions which are entered from a console. If this is the case, one could manually enter the jump to the starting address of the system monitor and achieve the same result.

The system monitor which is included with the Intellec 8 microcomputer begins at address 3800. Therefore, to start this system monitor, one must load a JMP into word 0000, the low order portion of the address, 00, in word 0001, and the high order portion, 38, in word 0002. Therefore, the contents of memory would be

0000	C3
0001	00
0002	38
0003	••

Now, if the reset button is pushed, the computer will be forced to execute the "JMP 3800" command which has been stored in the first 3 memory locations. When the INTEL monitor starts, it types

8080 V3.0

Whenever it is ready to receive further instructions, it will type a • on the terminal.

The system monitor program will respond to a set of commands. These commands are usually given by typing a single letter on the terminal and following it with whatever additional information that particular command requires. In succeeding sections, we will examine the use of the monitor commands that are available on the INTEL monitor.

7.2 Displaying and Changing Memory

One of the principal features of a system monitor is that it allows us easily to display and change the contents of memory locations. To display the hexadecimal contents of a location, we simply type an S, followed immediately by the address of the location we are interested in, followed by a space. The computer will respond by typing the contents of the location in hexadecimal, followed by a minus sign. Using bold face letters to indicate what the user types and regular letters to indicate what the computer types, this would look like

> •**S0000b**C3-

We have used a **b** to indicate the blank typed by the user. After typing the contents of the location, the computer will wait for further instructions from the user. Assuming that we do not wish to change the contents of this memory location, we may do one of two things:

1) Type a carriage return (indicated by an **r**). This will "close" the current location and return the control to the monitor program. The monitor will respond by typing a line feed (indicated by an f) and then typing a period. It is now ready for further commands.

2) Type a blank. This will close the current location and display the contents of the next memory location in sequence.

Let's return to the preceding example and show what would happen if we typed a blank.

> •**S0000b**C3-**b**00-

Here the monitor has responded to our request by typing the contents 00 of the next memory location, location number 0001. The procedure can be repeated to display as many words as we wish.

If we wish to change the contents of a memory location that has been displayed, we simply type the desired contents in hexadecimal and follow that with either a blank or a carriage return. Again, returning to our example, suppose that we wished to change the destination of the jump instruction from 3800 to 271F. The dialog with the computer would now be

> •**S0001b**00-**1Fb**38-**27r**f
> •

We have indicated with the f that the computer responds to our carriage-return (r) with a line-feed (f).

The system monitor and the S command are very convenient for loading a program into memory. Suppose that we wish to enter the following program beginning at location 0100.

Location	Code	Instruction	Comment
0100	DB	IN 02	READ SWITCHES
0101	02		
0102	D3	OUT 0B	LIGHT LIGHTS
0103	0B		
0104	C3	JMP 0100	LOOP BACK
0105	00		
0106	01		

We could do this in the following manner. (Remember that we type everything that is in bold face, the computer types everything else.)

•**S0100**b00-**DB**b00-**02**b00-**D3**b00-**0B**b00-**C3**b00-**b**00-**01**rf
•

Of course, the line which is actually typed on the terminal will not have bold face or lowercase letters in it. What you will see when you are through will look like

•S0100 00-DB 00-02 00-D3 00-0B 00-C3 00-00-01
•

The S instruction is referred to as the *substitute* command and it is a very easy way to make small changes to the contents of memory.

7.3 Transfering Control
The system monitor can also be used to transfer control to any location. This is accomplished by means of the Go command. The Go command causes a JMP to the address specified by the command. Therefore, to transfer control to location 0000 one would type

•**G0000**rf

If this command were executed immediately after entering the system monitor, the jump to the system monitor command would still be present at location 0000. Therefore, the computer will re-enter the monitor and it will respond with its opening line. The terminal device will print

> •G0000
> 8080 V3.0

Consider, now, running the program which reads the switches and lights the lights. In the previous section, we described how to enter this program beginning at word 0100. Therefore, to start the program, one would simply type

> **•G0100**rf

If one did this, the computer would begin to execute the light and switch program.

In order to return to the system monitor, one could simply push the reset button. If we assume that we have not changed the contents of memory locations 0000, 0001, and 0002, they would still contain the jump to the system monitor.

The ability to return control to the system monitor by pushing the reset button is very convenient. If one makes an error while entering a program, the program can do many strange things. It is desirable, therefore, to have an ability to return to the system monitor at any time. As a result, it is advisable to always store the jump to the system monitor command in the three words starting at word 0000 and not to use these locations for anything else.

It is, of course, possible to have the program jump directly to the system monitor. For example, if we redo our earlier example to have the computer read the switches, light the lights and return to the system monitor, the program would look like

Location	Code	Instruction		Comment
0100	DB	IN	02	READ SWITCHES
0101	02			
0102	D3	OUT	0B	LIGHT LIGHTS
0103	0b			
0104	C3	JMP	3800	JUMP TO MONITOR
0105	00			
0106	38			

The only change that needs to be made in the earlier program is in the contents of word 0106. It needs to be changed from 01 to 38. To do so one simply types

> •**S0106b**01-**38**rf

Now, if you type

> •**G0100**rf

the computer will read the switches, light the lights, and return to the system monitor.

7.4 Displaying Registers

As we have seen, the system monitor program is capable of displaying and changing the contents of memory locations. There are times, however, when we wish to know what the computer is actually storing in its registers. Therefore, monitors generally provide a method for accessing this information. In the INTEL monitor, for example, it is possible to have the monitor store these registers and display them using the X command.

In order to have the monitor save the register contents, it must be entered in a special way. Instead of performing a JMP 3800, one must perform a CALL 3F08. The code for the CALL instruction is CD. It is almost the same as a JMP instruction but it has an additional feature. We shall discuss this instruction in some detail in Chapter 11; for now, however, we will assume that it is just a special form of JMP.

When the system monitor program is entered at location 3F08, several things happen. The contents of the registers are stored in special memory locations and the terminal device prints an asterisk, followed by the number of the location just beyond the last byte of the CALL instruction. Thus, if you had CALL 3F08 at several places in a program, you would know which one was used.

In order to find out what the contents of the registers are, one uses the X command. This is essentially the same as the S command, except that it refers to registers rather than to memory locations. To find out the contents of register A, one types XA. The computer will respond by typing a space followed by the hexadecimal representation for the contents of the A register at the time the CALL instruction was executed and then a dash. To find out the contents of register B, one need only type a space and the computer will respond by typing what was in B. In fact, by continually pushing the space bar, one can determine the contents of all registers.

To illustrate the use of the X instruction, consider the following program:

Location	Code	Instruction		Comment
0100	3E	MVI	A,12	MOVE 12 INTO A
0101	12			
0102	06	MVI	B,34	MOVE 34 INTO B
0103	34			
0104	0E	MVI	C,56	MOVE 56 INTO C
0105	56			
0106	57	MOV	D,A	MOVE A INTO D
0107	58	MOV	E,B	MOVE B INTO E
0108	CD	CALL	3F08	CALL MONITOR
0109	08			
010A	3F			

We will load this program using the S instruction. If we have not changed the computer from our previous example, the sequence of steps will be

> •S0100bDB-3Eb01-12b1F-06bDA-34b00-0Eb01-
> 56bDB-57b00-58bD3-CDb00-08b32-3Frf
> •

Now, when we run the program, it will fill A and D with 12, B and E with 34 and C with 56. To run it, we transfer control to 0100. The terminal will print

> •G0100
> *010B
> •

The monitor told us that it was called by the instruction in the three locations which preceded 010B. To determine if the program worked, we can use X to examine the register contents. We type

> •XAb 12-b34-b56-b 12-b34-rf
> •

The X command also lets us alter the contents of the register. To do so, we just enter the new data after the minus sign. Thus, if we type

> •XAb12-ABb34-CDRf
> •

and run the program starting at 0106

>   •**G0106**rf
>   *010B
>   •

the D and E register will contain AB and CD. To show that they do, we again use X

>   •**XA**b AB-**b**CD-**b**56-**b**AB-**b**CD-**rf**
>   •

In addition to the registers that we are familiar with, the X command can be used to examine others. A complete list of the registers accessed by X is as follows:

>   A register
>   B register
>   C register
>   D register
>   E register
>   F flags (including the zero flag)
>   H register
>   L register
>   HL register pair
>   PC program counter
>   SP stack pointer (see Chapter 11)

7.5 Breakpoints

As you know if you have done any computer programming, it is very difficult to get a program to run right the first time. In fact, you usually spend a lot more time fixing, or debugging, a program than you do writing it. To debug a microprocessor program, it is frequently useful to stop it in the middle and see what is going on. One way to do this is to put a CALL 3F08 wherever you wish to stop the program. Another way is to use *breakpoints.*

When you tell the system monitor to *set a breakpoint* at a certain memory location, it essentially puts a CALL 3F08 command at that location. Then, if the program ever gets to that location, it jumps to the system monitor and you can see what was happening.

As with the other topics in this chapter, the details of setting breakpoints vary between monitors. In fact, many monitors do not have breakpoints. For the INTEL monitor, one sets the breakpoints as part of the G command. To set a breakpoint at 010A in a program that starts at 0100, one would type

>   •**G0100**b**010A**rf

the program ever gets to 010A, the terminal prints

>   *010A
>   •

Note that for a breakpoint, the monitor types the actual location of the breakpoint, not some location following it. Thus, a breakpoint is not exactly the same as CALL 3F08.

.6 Other Monitor Commands

Most system monitors can do many other things besides those described above. In this section, we will look at several of those features that are common, and indicate the other areas where system monitors are useful.

As we shall see later, it is very desirable to load the program into the computer from long-term storage media. For example, permanently storing programs on punched paper tape or magnetic tape enables us to greatly simplify many computer programming tasks. Therefore, all system monitors are equipped to read such programs. Since punched paper tape is the simplest such medium to describe, we will assume that the computer system we use in our examples is equipped with it.

All long-term storage media, like paper tape, store both the program itself and information about where it is to be located in memory. Therefore, in order to load the program, the system monitor need only be told to read the information. Thus, the command on the INTEL system is simply the letter R followed by a carriage return. This command will read a paper tape and place the information in the appropriate memory locations. It will continue until it reaches the end of the tape and then it will return control to the monitor.

In addition to the ability to read paper tapes, system monitors are usually able to create paper tapes. This is a more complex process and we will not describe it in detail here. The user is usually required to tell the computer first to punch blank paper tape, then to punch the desired information, then to punch an end of tape indicator, and finally to punch some more blank tape. This process may require that the user turn the punch on and off many times in order to record only the desired information.

Some system monitors are written to use audio tape cassettes instead of punched paper tape. Again, this is a more complex process and we will only describe it in general. The added difficulty with magnetic tapes is that one tape may contain many *files.* Each file will be one program. The monitor must be able to locate the correct file on the tape and then load it. Thus, some system of labeling segments of the tape must be used.

Other features of a system monitor may include the ability to control a PROM programmer, commands to transfer blocks of memory, an instruction to print large segments of memory at one time and the capability of assisting with input/output operations. These features vary from computer to computer and are best learned by consulting the instruction manuals that accompany each computer.

7.7 Exercises

1) Write a program to store the hexadecimal numbers 00 through FF in words 0600 through 06FF. When the program is finished, it should return control to the system monitor. Write this program on a piece of paper with both the instruction names and instruction codes. If you have a computer available, start your system monitor and use it to load and run the program. Check your work by being certain that the words from 0600 through 06FF actually contain the correct values.

2) Write a program that will input a number from the thumb wheel unit and fill that many locations on page 7 with the number.

8 USE OF TERMINAL FOR INPUT AND OUTPUT

As noted in Chapter 7, most microcomputer installations have some sort of terminal device available. Such a device consists of a typewriter-like keyboard for entering information and some sort of display mechanism. The terminal may display information by printing it on paper or by showing it on a TV-like screen. Although the keyboard and display elements may physically be in the same enclosure, the computer considers them as separate entities. The keyboard acts as an input device while the printer is an output device. These two devices are generally not connected together to operate as a typewriter unless a program is written to do so. (See Section 10.5.)

In this chapter, we will describe how the computer can read information from the keyboard of the terminal device and write information on the printer. As we shall see, this is only a little bit more complicated than reading switches and lighting lights.

8.1 ASCII Code

Each key on the terminal keyboard has an 8-bit (1 byte) code associated with it. This code is used by the computer to represent that key. A table of some of these codes is given below; a more complete table is contained in Appendix C.

This code is known as the ASCII code, which stands for American Standard Code for Information Interchange. You may note that on your terminal keyboard, some keys have more than one symbol. The second or upper symbol is obtained by holding down the SHIFT or CNTRL key while striking the key.

TABLE 8.1   ASCII Code.

Character	ASCII	Character	ASCII	Character	ASCII
0	30	D	44	Q	51
1	31	E	45	R	52
2	32	F	46	S	53
3	33	G	47	T	54
4	34	H	48	U	55
5	35	I	49	V	56
6	36	J	4A	W	57
7	37	K	4B	X	58
8	38	L	4C	Y	59
9	39	M	4D	Z	5A
A	41	N	4E	Space	20
B	42	O	4F	Line Feed	0A
C	43	P	50	Car Ret	0D

Whenever the computer reads an input from a terminal device, the ASCII code for the key that is pressed is transferred into the A register. Similarly, whenever we wish to print a given character on the terminal printer, we must place the ASCII code for that character in the A register.

There is one problem that occasionally arises when using ASCII code. The code is actually a seven-bit code with an eighth bit added. Therefore, this eighth bit can be arbitrary. Note that in the table, if one wrote out the binary form of the code for any letter, the leftmost, or high-order, bit is always zero. This need not always be the case. In fact, some terminals are set to always give a one in the leftmost bit. Others use the leftmost bit to set the *parity* of the word. That is, they fix it so that there are always an even (or odd, in some terminals) number of ones in the word by adjusting the leftmost bit. There are even some terminals that let the user determine the eighth bit for himself.

Many computers have their programs written to ignore the leftmost or parity bit. We will see in the next section that this is fairly easy to do.

8.2 Input from the Keyboard
We are now ready to discuss inputting data from the terminal keyboard. When a key is pressed on the keyboard, the terminal actually generates the eight-bit ASCII code in *sequence,* i.e., one bit after the other. The computer needs to read all eight bits in parallel or all at the same time. Therefore, it must have a special interface that collects all eight bits and presents them to the computer. (See Section 15.4.)

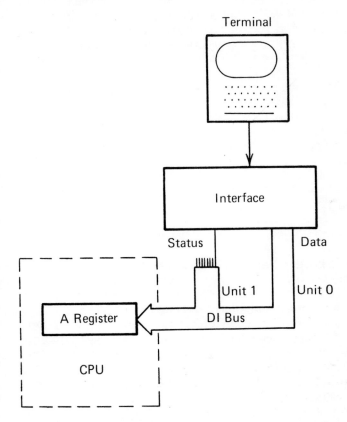

Figure 8.1 Input from the terminal.

When the interface has eight bits ready to send, it prepares a signal for the computer and it waits. If the computer wants to read a character from the keyboard, it must first check this signal, or *status* bit to see if there is information available. For the Intellec 8, the input status bit is the rightmost, or least significant bit on input unit 1.

The computer can obtain this status bit by using the following code:

```
DB      IN 1
01
```

This instruction causes the terminal status word to be transferred into the A register. The *data available* (DA) bit is the least significant bit in this word. When that bit is equal to zero, there is a character available for input, when it is a one, there is not.

Therefore, inputting data from the terminal is a two-step process: first, the processor must check to see if data is available and then it has to read the data. The data itself comes into the computer on a separate input unit. For the Intellec 8, it is unit 0. The system structure is shown in Fig. 8.1.

Before we can write a program to read from the terminal, we must find a way to determine whether a certain bit is a zero or a one. One obvious possibility is to mask off all of the other bits and to do a conditional jump based on the zero flag. To do the masking, we would do

ANI   01

This would set the seven leftmost bits of A to zero and leave the rightmost bit unchanged. (If you have trouble seeing this, try it on a piece of paper.) Now, if the DA bit were zero, the zero flag would be set; if it were a one, the flag would not be set.

As is often the case, there is a better way than the obvious one. To explain it, however, we must add another piece to the CPU. In addition to the registers and the zero flag, there is another one bit location. Its contents are called the Carry bit and are used in certain arithmetic operations. There are two things that make it useful for us now: a) There are two conditional jumps based on the Carry bit (JC and JNC) and b) The RRC instruction rotates bit a_0 into Carry as well as into a_7 (See Fig. 8.2.). Therefore, a complete program for inputting a character from the terminal takes the following form:

Location	Code	Instruction	Comment
0100	DB	IN 1	READ THE STATUS WORD
0101	01		
0102	OF	RRC	SHIFT DA BIT INTO CARRY
0103	DA	JC 0100	LOOP IF DA HIGH
0104	00		
0105	01		
0106	DB	IN 0	READ AVAILABLE DATA
0107	00		
0108	F6	ORI 80	SET PARITY BIT HI
0109	80		

The last instruction is added to insure that the leftmost bit a_7 is a "1". As noted in Appendix C, this bit is the *parity* bit and different terminals may set it in different ways. Therefore, we use the ORI 80 to avoid confusion.

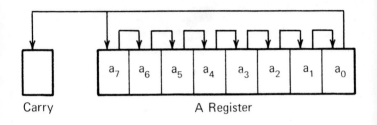

Figure 8.2 The RRC instruction.

The instruction IN 0 causes the actual input of the character into the A register once it has been determined that a character is available.

The JC instruction causes a jump to the location specified in bytes two and three if the Carry bit is set (i.e., if it is a 1). The RRC instruction rotates the a_0 bit, which is the DA bit, into the Carry bit position as well as into the a_7 position. If DA = 1, we execute the JC instruction and return to the beginning of the program. If, however, DA = 0, we do not jump and we execute the IN 0 instruction.

Some computers do something which can be confusing to the first time user. Instead of loading the ASCII code for a given key into the A register, they load the complement of the code. Thus, although the code for a Q is 51, the contents of the A register after a Q is pushed on the keyboard and read by the computer, would be AE. This is obviously an easy thing to take care of, it is just a little confusing. Our example machine, the Intellec 8, happens to be one that does this.

8.3 Output to the Printer
We must also use a status bit when outputting characters to the terminal printer. This status bit tells the computer that the printer is able to accept another character. It is necessary because the computer can produce output at a rate much faster than the terminal can print. The IN 01 command is again used to get this status information, but the bit of interest in this case is a_2 rather than a_0. If a_2 = 0, the printer is free and a character can be outputted.

The character to be printed is sent to the interface on output unit 00. The interface takes the eight bit message which arrives in parallel and sends it to the terminal in serial form. This is illustrated in Fig. 8.3.

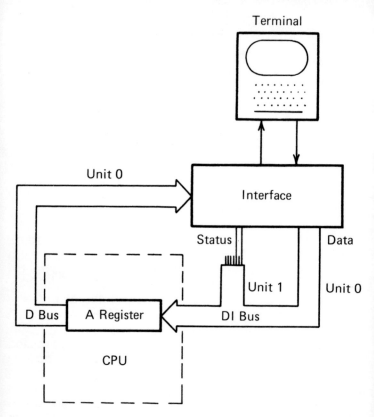

Figure 8.3 Output to the terminal.

The following code can be used to output a character to the printer. We assume that the ASCII code for the character to be printed has been placed in the B register.

Location	Code	Instruction		Comments
0100	DB	IN	01	READ STATUS WORD
0101	01			
0102	OF	RRC		PLACE STATUS
0103	OF	RRC		BIT IN
0104	OF	RRC		CARRY
0105	DA	JC	0100	LOOP IF TERMINAL
0106	00			IS BUSY
0107	01			
0108	78	MOV A,B		LOAD ASCII IN
0109	D3	OUT	00	PRINT CHARACTER
010A	00			

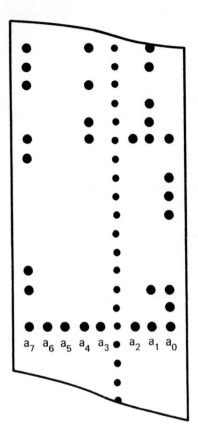

Figure 8.4 Punched paper tape.

Note that here we do three RRC's to move the a_2 bit into the Carry bit position.

Just as some computers complement the ASCII code on input, some (including the Intellec 8) complement it on output. For example, to print a Q using the above program on the Intellec 8, one must load AE into B.

8.4 Paper Tape Reader and Punch
Many microcomputers use punched paper tape for long term storage of data and programs. The tape itself is a heavy grade paper that is one inch wide. It represents binary information by using a hole to indicate a 1 and the lack of a hole to indicate 0. Typically, the tape is 8 bits wide so that a full byte can be written across the tape. Figure 8.4 shows a segment of the tape and the labels associated with each of

the 8 bits are indicated. The small holes are called *sprocket holes* and are used to guide the tape through the reader. Paper tape is an inexpensive long term storage medium, but it is somewhat bulky to handle.

One of the principal advantages of punched paper tape is that the devices which are used to punch it and read it are inexpensive. It is possible to purchase a new Model 33 Teletype complete with paper tape punch and reader for about $1200, and second-hand ones are even less. These units are fairly slow, however, and run at 10 characters per second. A character is the full 8 bits across the tape.

Higher speed units are available that will punch tape at 30 to 50 characters per second and read it at 200 or 300. These devices cost around $2000 and are found in many microcomputer installations.

The teletype tape reader sends characters to the computer in exactly the same way as the terminal keyboard. In fact, if the reader is turned on, the computer cannot tell if a character came from the reader or from the keyboard. Frequently, the teletypes connected to microcomputers are equipped with a relay that lets the computer turn the paper tape reader on and off. This relay is connected to the computer just like the lights on the light and switch box.

When the paper tape punch on a teletype is turned on, it is mechanically connected to the printer. Thus, any character that is printed is also punched, and vice versa. Therefore, if one wants to punch a tape and also print messages, the tape punch must be turned on and off at the right times. When using a teletype, one punches and reads paper tapes with the same programs used to print and read characters. The only change is that the reader and punch must be turned on. High speed readers and punches are almost identical. They have status bits just like the terminal does. The only difference is that they will use different unit codes.

8.5 Exercises

The purpose of these exercises is to make use of the terminal as an input and output device. Use the system monitor to enter and debug each program.

1) Write a program which will input a character from the terminal and display the associated ASCII code in the lights.

2) Write a program that will input a hexadecimal character code from the thumbwheels or the switch register and print the associated character on the terminal when the first switch in the Switch Register is turned on. Note that many hexadecimal numbers do not correspond to characters which print.

3) Write a program which will accept a character from the keyboard and will compare it ASCII code with the thumb-wheel or switch register setting. If the two match, type an "X"; if they do not match, type "O".

4) If you want to try something a little harder, write a program which will accept a string of characters and store them in memory until a carriage-return is received. After the carriage-return, type out the whole line followed by a carriage-return and line-feed.

9 **EDITORS**

9.1 Symbolic Assemblers and Editors

In all of the programs we have written so far, the programmer has been required to translate the instructions from their human readable form to a machine readable form. This is a laborious and uninteresting process and, when we are finished with it, we have a program that is very difficult for a human to read. To eliminate these hardships, the concept of an *Assembler* was evolved. This is a computer program which reads the human readable version of the program and translates it into a machine readable version.

In order for the assembler program to do its job, the computer must be able to read the symbolic version of the program. Therefore, the program must be written on some machine-readable medium. Typically, this is either punched paper tape, audio cassettes or the familiar computer cards. The hardware required to prepare and read computer cards is far more costly than that associated with punched paper tape or tape cassettes. Therefore, microcomputer systems normally use punched paper tape or audio tape.

If computer cards were used, it would be easy for a user to prepare and correct his program. He would punch each line of the program on a separate card and could correct any errors by replacing the card. On punched paper tape and audio tapes, however, this is not possible. Everything is on one piece of material and it is not easy to make substitutions. Therefore, it is necessary to have a computer program which enables the user to prepare an error-free tape. This program is called an *Editor*. It lets the user enter his program into the computer in symbolic form, make any changes or corrections, and prepare a punched paper tape or audio tape containing the complete final program. In fact, one can use the editor to prepare a tape of anything, not just computer programs.

For simplicity, this chapter and the next chapter will only describe paper tape editors and assemblers. We could just as easily talk about a system that uses magnetic tapes or a floppy disk drive, but the details of these latter systems are reserved for Chapter 15.

9.2 Basic Features

The editor is a special computer program for the microcomputer system that lets a user enter a string of text, correct any errors, list the text, and punch a paper tape of the corrected text. Generally, one uses an editor to prepare assembly level programs, i.e., problems still in symbolic or human readable form rather than machine readable form. However, the editor is like a typewriter and can be used to prepare any sort of information.

In addition to entering information, the editor can list it and change it. The user can list a single line or a sequence of lines. He can ask the program to change a certain line and, sometimes, he can even ask it to change only a part of a line.

Since the objective of an editor is to prepare a program for the computer, there must be some output device, such as a paper tape punch. An editor must be capable of preparing a proper punched paper tape for use by the assembler. This tape will contain the ASCII code for each character in the program, and is usually referred to as the *source tape*. In addition, most editors provide a facility for reading previously punched source tapes. This lets the user modify existing programs. Therefore, the set of editor commands must include certain tape handling operations.

There are a number of different types of editors; we will describe three. The first and simplest is a basic line-oriented editor. All data is entered into the editor as a full line, that is, a sequence of characters terminated by a carriage-return and line-feed.

Each line is numbered by the user when he types it and the computer stores the lines in numeric order. To change a line, the user would enter a new line with the same number and the computer would replace the old line with the new one. To add a new line at the end of a listing, the user gives it a higher number then the current last line.

If the lines are numbered consecutively (i.e., 1,2,3,4...) it will not be possible to insert new lines in the middle of the program. However, if they are numbered 10, 20, 30, 40...; new lines can be inserted anywhere, even at the beginning.

A basic line-oriented editor is a relatively simple program and, therefore, it is often used. Unfortunately, it is quite cumbersome to work with. The requirement to number each line and the need to retype an entire line to correct an error can be painful. However, if the editor is being used to write programs in BASIC (see Chapter 17), line numbers may be necessary and this simple form of editor can then be appropriate.

A second type of editor is the more complex line-oriented editor. It also stores information as complete lines but it does not require the user to number the lines. Instead, it utilizes an internal line numbering system. It refers to the first line as line 1, the second line as line 2, etc. Generally, it numbers lines using the decimal numbering system.

If one wishes to insert a line between lines 2 and 3, one can ask the editor to do so. The new line becomes line 3; the old line 3 automatically becomes 4, and so on. In this way, there is no limit on inserting lines anywhere in the program.

The most complex form of editor permits the user to address not only lines but also characters within a line. For example, one can use it to delete the fourth character of the third line of a program. In order to help the user keep track of what he is doing, such an editor usually makes use of a software pointer. This is an imaginary device which indicates where in the set of text the user is working. For example, if the user lists the fourth line of his program, the pointer will be pointing at the beginning of the fourth line. In order to list the fifth line, the computer can be instructed to list the line one step below the pointer rather than being given the exact line number. This is very useful in a long program when it is sometimes difficult to keep track of the number of the line upon which you are working.

9.3 The INTEL Editor

In this section, we will present an abbreviated list of the instructions in the INTEL editor. These instructions are all used in the example in the next section. Therefore, if you have difficulty understanding their meaning here, don't worry about it. The meanings should become clear in the next section when the instructions are actually used.

In this section and the next section, we will deal only with those editor instructions which operate on complete lines. In Section 9.5, we will present the instructions which deal with individual characters. These are a bit more complex but extremely useful.

All editor commands are one letter commands. They may be preceded or followed by additional information.

All editor commands are terminated by typing two ESCAPE characters. An ESCAPE character is generated by holding down the CTRL key and striking the key labeled ESCAPE or ALT MODE. If your terminal device does not have a key labeled this way, consult your manual to determine which set of keys will generate the ASCII code 7D.

A- The *Append* command. This command is used to read text from the paper tape reader. It is the command that you would use if you had already written a program which needed to be modified. Before the editor is given the append command, the tape must be loaded into the reader and the reader turned on. When this is done, simply type an A followed by two ESCAPE characters. The tape will be read and the editor will type an asterisk when the tape is finished.

I- The *Insert* command. This command is also used to input text to the editor. It will insert text at the location pointed to by the pointer. When it is finished, the pointer will point to the end of the new text. If you wanted to create a new program, you would type an I followed by the program. You would terminate each line of the program by hitting a carriage return and the editor would add the line feed. When you have finished typing your program and have terminated the last line with a carriage return, you would end the Insert procedure by typing two ESCAPE characters.

The next three commands all deal with moving the pointer. As the Insert command illustrated, the pointer position is critical to the operation of the other commands.

B- The *Beginning* command. This command causes the pointer to be moved to the beginning of the text. It is particularly useful when the user wishes to insert new information at the beginning of his program.

Z- The *End of the Text* command. The Z command moves the pointer to the end of the text. This is useful when the user wishes to add information at the end of his program.

L- The *Line* command. This command is used to move the pointer forward or backward in the text buffer a certain number of lines. If the command is just L, the pointer is moved one line forward. If the command is 3L, the pointer is moved three lines forward. If the command is -7L, the pointer is moved seven lines backward. The editor con-

siders a line to be a sequence of characters terminated
with a carriage return character.

- The *Kill* command. This command is used to delete lines
from your program. If the command is just K, the line to
which the pointer is pointing will be erased. If the
command were 3K, the three lines, beginning with that to
which the pointer is pointing, will be erased. If the command is -7K, the seven lines preceding the pointer will be
deleted.

- The *Type* command. This command is used to print data
on the terminal. As with K and L, the user can type one or
several lines. A simple T will just cause the current line to
be printed; 3T will cause the current line and the next two
lines to be printed; -7T will cause the seven lines
preceding the current line to be printed.

- The *End* command. This command is used when the user
is satisfied that what he has in his text buffer is what he
wishes to punch on tape. It causes all the text that the
computer now holds to be punched on tape and the tape
to be ended in an appropriate way and, finally, all the text
in the computer to be erased.

- The *Null* command. This command causes the computer
to punch six inches of blank tape. It is usually used before
the E command to produce a leader on the tape.

These commands are all used in the example of the next
section.

There are two other features of the editor about which
you should be aware. The first is the *rubout* key. This
enables you to delete erroneous characters. Pushing the
rubout key will erase the preceding character on the line you
are currently typing. Unfortunately, but unavoidably, it only
erases it inside the computer; it will still appear on your output device. This command is quite useful if you notice a
typing error as soon as it occurs. If you only notice it after
you have typed an entire line, it is best to use the K
command to delete your error.

The next feature is the *tab*. As does the tabulator on a
typewriter, this command lets the user put data in columns.
We shall see later that this command makes writing
programs in assembly language significantly easier. To use
the tab, you hold down the CNTL key and push the I. On
some keyboards, this key is labeled as TAB; but on others, it
is not.

9.4 Example
Suppose that we wish to make a source tape of the program

used in Section 7.2 to illustrate the system monitor. To d
so, we first need to load the editor into the computer. Th
method for doing so will depend on the computer bein
used. It will also depend on what type of paper tape reader
available. The procedure will be to start the system monito
and to give the command which reads from paper tap
Assuming that this has been done, one must then transfe
control to the starting address of the text editor. For th
INTEL editor, this is 0010. Therefore, one gives the comman

•**G0010rf**

to the monitor and the editor takes over. To show that it i
running correctly, it types an opening line such as

INTELLEC 8 TEXT EDITOR, VERSION 4.0
*

We are now ready to begin to load our program.

Since we are writing a new program, we have no pape
tape to load. Therefore, we use the Insert command. Sinc
there is no text in the computer, we need only type I and w
are ready to start. We enter the data immediately followin
the I and it will look like this:

```
•IIN 02      READ SWITCHES
OUT 0B      LIGHT LIGHTS
JMP 0100   LOOP BACK
$$
```

The two dollar signs show where the ESCAPE comman
was typed. The text buffer will now contain our program. T
make sure that it does, we can make a listing of th
program. To do so, we first move the pointer back to th
beginning of the buffer with a B command, and then typ
three lines using the T command. The following will appea
on our terminal:

```
*B$$
*3T$$
IN 02        READ SWITCHES
OUT OB      LIGHT LIGHTS
JMP 0100   LOOP BACK
*
```

Suppose now that we wish to change the first two line
so that the words READ and LIGHT are lined up with th
word LOOP. To do so, we first have to delete these two line
with the K command, and then insert the two modified line
again. Therefore, we first move the pointer to the top of th

uffer with a B command, then delete two lines using the 2K ommand and, finally, insert the new line starting with the I ommand. The following will appear on the terminal:

```
*B$$
*2K$$
*IIN 02        READ SWITCHES
OUT 0B         LIGHT LIGHTS
$$
*
```

To verify that this has been done properly, we can now list the text buffer again using the T command:

```
*3T$$
JMP 0100   LOOP BACK
*
```

Oops, something happened! The editor only listed the third line of the program. We forgot to move the pointer back to the beginning of the text buffer! Remember that, when the editor finishes the I command, it leaves the pointer at the end of the new information. Therefore, to list what we want to list, we must first use the B command. Doing so yields the following:

```
*B$$
*3T$$
IN 02        READ SWITCHES
OUT 0B       LIGHT LIGHTS
JMP 0100     LOOP BACK
*
```

Now, if we are satisfied with this information, we can punch a tape. To do so, we must first use the N command to generate blank tape at the front. The total output looks like:

```
*N$$
START PUNCH, TYPE CHAR
```

where the second line has been typed by the editor program. After turning on the teletype punch, we strike any character on the keyboard and a string of 6 inches of blank tape is generated. After the blank tape is punched, we must turn off the tape punch and strike another character to tell the editor that we are finished. It will respond with an asterisk. We are now ready to enter the E command which we terminate with two ESCAPE characters. The computer will again ask us to turn the punch on and we must do so. It will then punch and print the program.

```
*E$$
START PUNCH, TYPE CHAR
IN 02        READ SWITCHES
OUT 0B       LIGHT LIGHTS
JMP 0100     LOOP BACK
```

When it has finished punching the tape, it will again wait
This time it is waiting for us to turn the punch off. After we
turn the punch off and type a character, it will type its open
ing line and be ready for a new command. This is indicated
below:

INTELLEC 8 TEXT EDITOR, VERSION 4.0
    *

Now, suppose that we wish to alter the program so that it
jumps to the system monitor rather than to the beginning o
the loop. To do so, we must use the A command to read in
the tape that we have punched. After loading the tape into
the reader, we type the A command followed by two
ESCAPE characters. This just looks like:

    *A$$

The only way that we know so far to change a part of a line is
to kill the entire line and replace it with the new line. To point
at the line which we wish to change, we first use the Z
command to point at the end of the text buffer. Then, we
use the -1L command to move the pointer back one line
Before killing the line, we must make certain that we are in
the right place so we will use a T command. Finally, we will
delete the line with a K command and replace it using the
command. Our terminal at this point looks like the following

```
*A$$
*Z$$
*-1L$$
*T$$
JMP 0100        LOOP BACK
*K$$
*IJMP 3800      JUMP TO MONITOR
$$
```

If we wanted to, we could now punch this new program
using the N command to make a leader and then using the E
command.

9.5 Character Manipulations
In this section we will describe some character-oriented
features of the INTEL editor. These features are not found

on all editors and, consequently, may not be of importance to all users. They are included here only for those users who wish to know more about editors. If you don't, feel free to skip this section and go on to the next chapter.

All character manipulations are based on the location of the pointer which is used to indicate which line you are working on. It turns out that the pointer can actually be positioned between any two characters in the text buffer. Let us go back to the situation in the previous section where we have read in the tape using the A command. The pointer will be located after the line-feed which follows the third line.

The commands which will be of interest to us in manipulating characters are the following:

C- The *Character* command. This command is used to move the pointer either forward or backward a given number of characters. If it appears as just C, this means to move the pointer forward one character. If it appears as -14C, this means to move the pointer backward fourteen characters. Note that, when using this command, *all* characters are counted. This includes spaces, carriage-returns, and line-feeds.

D- The *Delete* command. This command is used to delete characters. As with the C command, it can be preceded by a number causing it to delete more than one character. For example, 7D will delete seven characters; and -12D will delete the twelve characters preceding the pointer. The pointer is unchanged.

F- The *Find* command. This command is used to find a string of up to 16 characters. To use it, one types F followed by the string to be found followed by two ESCAPE commands. The computer searches the text buffer starting at the pointer position to find this particular string of characters. If it finds it, it repositions the pointer at the *end* of the string. If it does not find it, it indicates this to the user and does not move the pointer.

S- The *Substitute* command. This command is quite useful but we defer it to the exercises. If you have mastered the preceding commands, you should have no difficulty in understanding this one.

As an example of using these character-oriented commands, let us re-do the problem of changing the destination of the jump in the third line of our example program. Assume that we have loaded the original program using the A command. The pointer is now at the end of the text buffer; that is, it follows the line feed after the third line. To move it to the beginning of the third line, we would use a -1L command. To verify the location of the pointer, we will use the T command. The result will look like the following:

```
*A$$
*-1L
*T$$
JMP 0100    LOOP BACK
*
```

Now we can move the pointer over to the beginning of the address portion of the JMP instructions by using the C command. If we then use the T command, it will type out the remaining portion of the line and show us that we are at the beginning of the address portion.

```
*4C$$
*T$$
0100  LOOP BACK
*
```

Now, we delete the next two characters using a 2D and verify that it worked again with the T command. We can now use the I command to insert the correct address. The command 0L will then move the pointer back to the beginning of the line and following this with a T command will show what the line now looks like.

```
*2D$$
*T$$
00    LOOP BACK
*I38$$
*0L$$
*T$$
JMP 3800    LOOP BACK
*
```

Note that the line is now correct.

Unfortunately, the comment is no longer pertinent. The instruction no longer does a LOOP BACK, it actually does a JUMP TO MONITOR. We could try to count how many characters there are between the beginning of the line and the comment and use C to move the pointer. It is easier, however, to use the F command to position the pointer at the beginning of the comment. We can then use the D command to remove the old comment and the C command to install the new one. The command sequence would look like this:

```
*FLOOP$$
*-4D$$
*5D$$
*IJUMP TO MONITOR$$
*B$$
*3T$$
IN 02        READ SWITCHES
OUT 0B       LIGHT LIGHTS
JMP 3800     JUMP TO MONITOR
*
```

We have concluded the example by listing the entire program as it now stands.

9.6 Exercises
1) If you have an editor program available to you, use it to prepare a machine readable copy of one of the programs contained in the text. You might, for example, do the simple three line program which we have been using in this chapter.
2) To show that you can use the editor for something other than preparing programs, use it to write a letter to a friend telling him how much fun you are having using your computer.
3) In addition to the single character commands described in Section 9.5, there is something called the S command. This command will Substitute a new string of characters for a given string. The general format is S followed by the old sequence of letters followed by an ESCAPE command followed by the new sequence of letters followed by two ESCAPE commands. How could we have used this in the example at the end of Section 9.5 to simplify the problem of changing the comment?

10

SYMBOLIC ASSEMBLERS

10.1 Instruction Format

The main purpose of the editor, introduced in Chapter 9, is as a tool which lets us use what is known as a *symbolic assembler.* The assembler is a program designed to automate the job of translating instructions from their symbolic names to their machine codes. In addition, it lets the user use convenient names to refer to memory locations, rather than having to use location numbers.

Throughout this book we have associated with each instruction both a name and a 2-digit hexadecimal number. The assembler has a dictionary which allows it to read the name of an instruction and associate the appropriate 2-digit code. It knows whether the instruction requires one, two or three memory locations. Therefore, when you use the assembler, you need no longer remember the hexadecimal code associated with each instruction.

Since an assembler is a computer program, its input must obey certain rules. If we do not follow these rules, the assembler will not properly interpret what we are trying to do. For example, each instruction presented to the assembler must occupy one line. This is true regardless of whether the instruction actually requires one, two or three words of memory. On this one line, you may put a location name if you will need to refer to a memory location and you may also put a comment to help you remember what the line means.

The general format of a line of assembly code is given below:

```
NAME:    INS    ARG    ;COMMENT
```

The first item in the line is the name which you assign to the machine location where the instruction begins. This name is easily identified because it is followed by a colon. If you do not wish to name the location, you may simply omit the first entry. The second entry is the name of the instruction. For example, an INput instruction would have the two letters IN as the second entry. The third entry is used to specify the argument for those instructions which require an argument. For example, the INput instruction must contain the number of the unit that is being used for input. Therefore, if you are inputting from the switch register, this third entry would be the number 2. The final entry, or comment, is any information which will be helpful to the programmer. The assembler stops reading a line when it encounters the semicolon. It essentially ignores anything that follows the semicolon. Therefore, you may put in the comment anything which will be hlepful to you in remembering how your program was supposed to work. For example, if you instruction reads the first data point by inputting from the switches, the total instruction might read as follows:

IN   02   ;INPUT FIRST DATA WORD

The space between entries is ignored by the assembler. Therefore, you may space things out in any way that is convenient.

10.2 Location Names and Instruction Mnemonics

In addition to using symbolic names rather than codes for instructions, the assembler is willing to use names for machine locations. As you saw when we were discussing JMP instructions, it is necessary to know the exact location of an instruction in memory in order to jump to it. Therefore, we had to figure out exactly where each instruction would be stored in memory before we could fill in the destination of the jumps. With an assembler, it is possible to give a name to a location and use this name, rather than the location number, as the argument of the jump instruction. The assembler will determine where everything goes and eventually fill in the correct location number.

There are several rules which you must follow if the assembler is to interpret your location names correctly:
a) Each location name must begin with a letter.
b) The name may be no more than five characters long. Except for the first character, the characters may be either numbers or letters.

c) The name must not be the same as the name of some instruction. You must be slightly careful of this requirement since you have not yet seen all of the instruction names. If you do run into a problem, check the complete assembly language listing in Appendix A to see whether a location name happens to match an instruction name.

d) The name must be separated from the rest of the instruction with a colon.

The word mnemonic (the first m is silent) means something that helps one to remember something else. Therefore, the symbolic instruction names which we have been using are referred to as mnemonic instructions. Although it may appear that we have just made them up as we went along, that is definitely not true. The mnemonics that we have used are part of a well defined set that is used by almost all 8080 assemblers. The tables in Appendix A and B list all of the 8080 mnemonic instructions.

10.3 Pseudo-Operations and Data

In addition to the instructions we are already familiar with, the assembler has certain other features. These are not regular computer operations and, therfore, are called pseudo-operations or pseudo-ops. They vary from assembler to assembler and we will not discuss them all. Two pseudo-ops, which are of particular interest for us, are the ones which indicate where the program should be stored and when the program is ended.

When the assembler assembles a program, it simply stores each successive instruction in the next available memory location. It is useful, therefore, to tell it where to put the first instruction. For example, if you wish to have you program begin in word 0100, you must tell that to the assembler. To do so, the first line in your program should read:

ORG 0100

This will cause the computer to store the next instruction in word 0100, so that the program will have its ORiGin at 0100.

To tell the assembler that it has seen the last instruction of the program, you need the pseudo-op END. As soon as the assembler reads a line which uses END instead of a standard instruction, it will assume that it has seen the entire program.

There are usually other pseudo-ops that an assembler will recognize. They are useful but not essential. Therefore, we will not discuss them here. When you use an assembler, it will be worth your while to find out what other pseudo-ops are available.

Some of the instructions have arguments which are data. For example,

> MVI   A,02

would load the A register with 02. The assembler requires that we obey the following two rules when we specify hexa-decimal data:

a) The data must begin with a numeric character — not a letter.

b) The data must be followed by an H.

Thus, if we want to load A with 02, the instruction would be

> MVI   A,02H

Suppose we wanted to load B with F3. Since F3 begins with a letter, we seem to have a problem. The solution is to use the instruction

> MVI   B,0F3H

The leading zero tells the assembler that it is dealing with numeric data but it does not change the value of the data.

The unit number for the Light Register is B. In order for the command to output A to the Light Register to be proper-ly interpreted, we must write it as

> OUT   0BH

Most assemblers are willing to deal with other types of data. Usually it is possible to enter data in decimal, octal, binary and ASCII form. The details of doing so can be a bit confusing the first time through, so we will not present them here.

10.4 Operation of an Assembler

The principal job of an assembler is to take a tape that con-tains a program written in a way that people can read it, and then create a tape with the program written so that the machine can run it. The first tape is the source tape gener-ated by the editor. It contains the ASCII representation of all of the characters in the program listing.

The tape produced by the assembler is called the *object tape*. It contains the instruction codes for the program, and the system monitor can load it directly into memory for execution. The object tape may contain either the ASCII representation of the hexadecimal instruction code or the binary form of the instruction code. In addition, it contains some sort of information on where to store the data.

Now that we know what an assembler is supposed to do, we shall analyze how it can do it. It might seem that it could just read each line and generate the appropriate hexadecimal code. Unfortunately, this is not quite the case. Remember that in addition to using instruction mnemonics, we are also using location names. Thus, the assembler must figure out where all of the instructions go before it can assign the appropriate location codes to each location name.

The need to decode the location names leads to the concept of a *two-pass assembler.* The assembler goes through the program twice; once to find out where everything belongs and a second time to replace location names with location codes. For most assemblers this means they have to read the source tape at least two times. As we shall see, they sometimes read it more than twice.

10.5 Example
The use of the assembler is best illustrated by an example. As before, we will use the INTEL software. Suppose you wish to write a computer program so that your terminal will act like a typewriter. Basically, what you need to do is have the computer read which key was pushed on the keyboard and echo it back to the printer. There is one additional feature which must be added. If the user pushes the "carriage-return" character, the computer should respond with both the "carriage-return" character and the "line-feed" character.

When writing any program, you should first list what functions your program must perform. For the present example, there would be three:
1) Read a character.
2) Print that character.
3) If that character was "carriage-return", also print "line-feed".

A program which will perform the three functions is given in Table 10.1.

This is what a listing prepared by the editor would look like. We have used the "tab" feature to place the information in columns. If an instruction had a location name, we hit "tab" after typing the name. If it had no name, we hit "tab" anyway. We used the "tab" after the instruction mnemonic and after the argument. As noted above, the assembler ignores this spacing but it makes it much easier for us to read the listing.

TABLE 10.1 Typewriter Program.

```
        ORG   0100H
LOP1:   IN    1          ;GET TERMINAL STATUS
        RRC              ;PUT STATUS BIT IN CARRY
        JC    LOP1       ;LOOP IF NO DATA
        IN    0          ;INPUT CHARACTER
        MOV   B, A        ;STORE IT IN B
LOP2:   IN    1          ;GET TERMINAL STATUS
        RRC              ;PUT PRINTER
        RRC              ;STATUS BIT
        RRC              ;IN CARRY
        JC    LOP2       ;LOOP IF BUSY
        MOV   A, B        ;GET CHARACTER
        OUT   0          ;PRINT IT
        CPI   72H        ;COMPARE 'CARRIAGE-RETURN'
        JNZ   LOP1       ;LOOP IF NOT 'CR'
LOP3:   IN    1          ;GET TERMINAL STATUS
        RRC              ;PUT PRINTER
        RRC              ;STATUS BIT
        RRC              ;IN CARRY
        JC    LOP3       ;LOOP IF BUSY
        MVI   A, 0F5H     ;LOAD 'LINE-FEED'
        OUT   0          ;OUTPUT 'LF'
        JMP   LOP1       ;START AGAIN
        END
```

Note that each instruction appears on one line of the program. The first line of the program uses the ORG pseudo-op to indicate that the program should begin in word 0100. Each succeeding line contains a location name (if needed), the instruction, the argument (if needed), and a comment indicating what the instruction does.

A careful examination will show that the program does achieve the three objectives outlined above. It first waits in the loop at the top of the program for a character to appear on the teletype. When the character appears, it reads it and stores it in register B.

The next job is to be certain that the teletype printer is available to accept a character. The loop labeled LOP2 does this. When the printer is free, the input character is returned to the A register from the B register and printed. The program then determines if a "carriage-return" was pushed. It compares the *complement* of the ASCII code for "carriage-return" to the contents of the A register, and jumps to the beginning of the program if the character was not a "carriage-return". Note that we have assumed that the parity bit a_7 will be "0" in the complement.

If a "carriage-return" was entered, the computer must output a "line-feed". To do this, it first waits in LOP3 until the teletype printer is free. It then loads the A register with the complement of the ASCII code for a "line-feed". It outputs the character and then returns to the beginning of the program.

The final line of the program is the psuedo-op END and it is used to indicate to the assembler that the program is complete.

Once you have written your program as above, you will want to have the assembler read it and generate the machine compatible program. The first step is to use the editor to punch a paper tape that contains everything that the program listing above has in it. The procedure that you follow in doing this has already been described in Chapter 9.

The next step is to load the assembler and have it assemble your program. The assembler is loaded using the R command from the system monitor just as the editor was, and is started by transferring control to word 0010. When the assembler program begins, it will type an opening label and then a P followed by an equal sign.

8080 MACRO ASSEMBLER, VERSION 3.0

P =

The first task that you want it to perform is to read your tape and determine where your instructions will be stored in memory. To do so, you load your source tape in the reader and type a "1". After you have typed the 1, the computer will read the tape until it comes to the END pseudo-op. During this first pass, the assembler will assign memory locations to each of your instructions. Therefore, it will be able to make a table of all of your location names together with their actual machine location.

During the next assembler pass, the assembler will assign codes to each of the instructions and arguments. To run the second pass, you must again place your source tape in the reader and type a "2". The assembler will print a detailed listing of your program together with a list of the machine representations of all of your instructions and their locations. In addition, it will indicate whether you have any obvious errors. If you do get error indicators, you should stop at this point and figure out what is wrong. Although the assembler will probably not find all of the errors, the ones it does find cannot be ignored.

TABLE 10.2 Assembler Listing.

```
0000                    ORG    0100H
0100   DB01   LOP1:     IN     1          ;GET TERMINAL STATUS
0102   0F               RRC               ;PUT STATUS BIT IN CARRY
0103   DA0001           JC     LOP1       ;LOOP IF NO DATA
0106   DB00             IN     0          ;INPUT CHARACTER
0108   47               MOV    B, A       ;STORE IT IN B
0109   DB01   LOP2:     IN     1          ;GET TERMINAL STATUS
010B   0F               RRC               ;PUT PRINTER
010C   0F               RRC               ;STATUS BIT
010D   0F               RRC               ;IN CARRY
010E   DA0901           JC     LOP2       ;LOOP IF BUSY
0111   78               MOV    A, B       ;GET CHARACTER
0112   D300             OUT    0          ;PRINT IT
0114   FE72             CPI    72H        ;COMPARE 'CARRIAGE-RETURN'
0116   C20001           JNZ    LOP1       ;LOOP IF NOT 'CR'
0119   DB01   LOP3:     IN     1          ;GET TERMINAL STATUS
011B   0F               RRC               ;PUT PRINTER
011C   0F               RRC               ;STATUS BIT
011D   0F               RRC               ;IN CARRY
011E   DA1901           JC     LOP3       ;LOOP IF BUSY
0121   3EF5             MVI    A, 0F5H    ;LOAD 'LINE-FEED'
0123   D300             OUT    0          ;OUTPUT 'LF'
0125   C30001           JMP    LOP1       ;START AGAIN
0000                    END
```

For our example, the actual program listing is shown in Table 10.2. The first column on the left shows the beginning location number for each instruction. The next column contains the hexadecimal representation of each instruction and any arguments it has. Thus, the first instruction, IN 1, is stored in locations 0100 and 0101 as DB and 01. The listing is extremely useful since it presents the program in both machine readable and human readable form.

If you and the assembler are satisfied with your listing, you are ready to prepare your object tape. Put your source tape back in the reader and turn the punch on. After turning the punch on, type a "3". The 3 will be punched on the tape, but this will not be a problem. The computer will now read the source tape on the reader and punch an object tape on the punch. If you are using a teletype, the punch and printer will be physically connected and you will get a listing of your tape. For our example, this is shown in Table 10.3. Compare this to the listing in Table 10.2 and see if you can figure out where the instruction codes are.

After these three passes, you will have both a detailed listing of your program and also an object tape that can be loaded directly into the computer. To read your object tape, first return to the system monitor by pushing RESET. Then, load your object tape into the reader and give an R command to the system monitor. The computer will then read the object tape and store the program in memory. To

TABLE 10.3 Object Tape Listing.

$

10010000DB010FDA0001DB0047DB010F0F0FDA091B
100110000178D300FE72C20001DB010F0F0FDA1964
080120000013EF5D300C300010C
000000001FF

$=

>egin program execution, you must simply transfer control,
using the G command, to the first word of your program.

0.6 Exercises
f you have an assembler available, the following exercises
will help you become familiar with it.
)) Repeat the example of Section 10.5. Your first time using
an assembler should be with a program that you know
works. You will make enough mistakes without trying
something fancy.
2) Do some of the exercises from Chapter 8. In particular,
see if you can do Exercise 4.

11 STACKS AND SUBROUTINES

11.1 Stack and Stack Operations

In this chapter, we examine one of the important features of the 8080 — the *stack* — and its use in writing programs. In particular, two new classes of instructions — *calls* and *returns* — will be introduced.

The stack consists of a block of sequential memory locations. Since we will wish both to read and to write in these locations, they must be in RAM memory. The stack on the 8080 uses the last-in-first-out (LIFO) method. In other words, the last thing that was placed on the stack is the first thing taken off. A helpful analogy is a vertical stack of books where all additions and removals take place at the top of the stack.

When data is stored in the stack, it is said to be *pushed* down onto the stack; when data is read from the stack, it is said to be *popped* up from the stack. In the 8080 microprocessor, data is always pushed or popped in two-byte quantities. There are four PUSH instructions as shown in Table 11.1. Each of these instructions causes the contents of two registers to be placed onto the stack. The Program Status Word (PSW) consists of the A register and the Flag register which contains the status of all condition flags such as the zero flag and the carry flag.

TABLE 11.1 PUSH Instructions.

Code	Instruction	Operation
C5	PUSH B	PUSH B and C Registers onto Stack
D5	PUSH D	PUSH D and E Registers onto Stack
E5	PUSH H	PUSH H and L Registers onto Stack
F5	PUSH PSW	PUSH Program Status Word onto Stack

There is a similar set of four POP instructions as shown in Table 11.2. Each of these instructions causes the last two bytes on the stack to be popped off and loaded into the appropriate register pair. Note that all of the PUSH and POP instructions are one-byte instructions.

TABLE 11.2 POP Instructions.

Code	Instruction	Operation
C1	POP B	POP B and C Registers off Stack
D1	POP D	POP D and E Registers off Stack
E1	POP H	POP H and L Registers off Stack
F1	POP PSW	POP Program Status Word off Stack

A sixteen-bit register, known as the Stack Pointer (SP), contains the memory address of the last item that was pushed onto the stack. When a register pair is pushed onto the stack, the Stack Pointer is decremented by two; when a register pair is popped from the stack, the Stack Pointer is incremented by two. The location of the stack is initially determined by setting the Stack Pointer using the instruction:

> 31   LXI SP, PPWW
> WW
> PP

This instruction causes the Stack Pointer to be set to page PP and word WW. The stack is usually located at or near the top (largest value) of RAM memory.

To illustrate the use and operation of the stack, let us consider the program given in Table 11.3. After the Stack Pointer

TABLE 11.3 Use of Stack Operation.

Location	Code	Instruction	Comment
0000	31	LXI SP, 06FF	;INITIALIZE STACK POINTER
0001	FF		
0002	06		
. . .		. . .	. . .
00F6	E5	PUSH H	;PUSH HL ONTO STACK
00F7	C5	PUSH B	;PUSH BC ONTO STACK
. . .		. . .	. . .
0111	C1	POP B	;POP BC OFF OF STACK
. . .		. . .	. . .

has been initialized, the system status is as shown in Fig. 11.1. Later in the program, the register pair HL is pushed onto the stack and the system status is then as shown in Fig. 11.2. Note that the contents of the H register are in memory location 06FE and the contents of L are in 06FD. Note also that H and L are unchanged. The Stack Pointer has been decremented by two and is now equal to 06FD, the last location used. Next the BC register pair is pushed onto the stack, leading to the system status as shown in Fig. 11.3.

Later in the program, the system status is as shown by Fig. 11.4. Note that the contents of all of the registers have changed. We now wish to restore the BC register pair by popping them off of the stack. The result of this operation is shown in Fig. 11.5. Note that SP has been increased by two.

When using stack operations, it is important to keep track of the order in which things are pushed onto the stack so

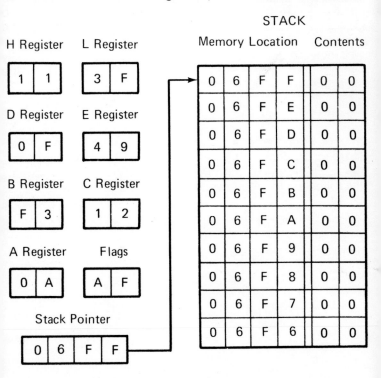

Figure 11.1 System status after initialization of stack pointer.

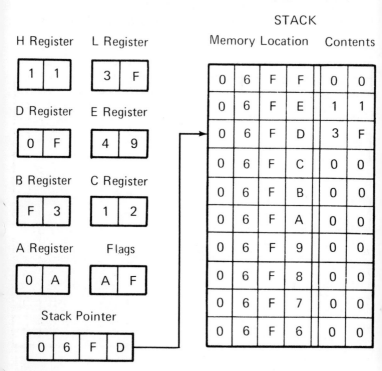

Figure 11.2 System status after PUSH H command.

that they may be correctly popped off. Ordinarily the POP instructions occur in the reverse order of the PUSH instructions. To store and then retrieve the BC and HL registers,
the following instruction sequence would be followed:

        PUSH B
        PUSH H
        ••••
        POP H
        POP B

If we use the instruction sequence

        PUSH B
        PUSH H
        ••••
        POP B
        POP H

then the HL and BC register pair contents will be inter-
changed. Of course, this may be the desired result in some
cases. It is important that stack operations always take

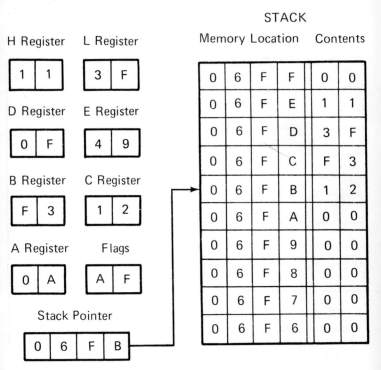

Figure 11.3 System status after PUSH B command.

place in pairs. For every PUSH instruction, there should be a corresponding POP. Otherwise, operations on the stack can exceed the memory allocated to it and destroy parts of the program or useful data.

11.2 CALL and RETurn Instructions
In writing a program, one often finds that a particular sequence of instructions is used repeatedly. For example, in a program which interacts with a terminal device, it is often necessary to read and write characters at several points in the program. Repetition of the complete set of instructions at each point can consume a great deal of memory. There is a way around this problem, namely the use of a subroutine.

Subroutines enable the computer to use a sequence of instructions in several places in a program without actually repeating the instructions. Consider for example the program of Table 10.1. This program makes the teletype act like a typewriter. Note that the sequence of instructions beginning at location LOP2 and continuing for six lines, is almost identical with that beginning at LOP3. In both cases, the

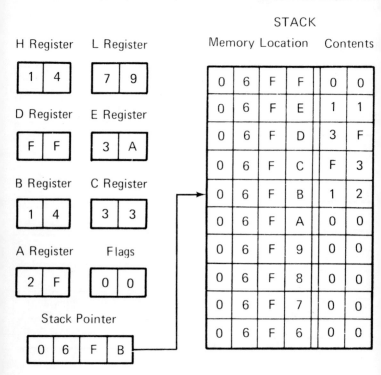

Figure 11.4 Later in the program.

computer determines the teletype status, waits for the printer to be free, loads the accumulator with an output character, and then sends it to the teletype.

The CALL command enables the user to do both of these jobs with half as many instructions. CALL can be thought of as a JMP command for which the computer remembers where it came from. The computer can return to this place in the program by using a RETurn command. Thus, it is possible to CALL a sequence of instructions from one place in a program and afterward RETurn to that place. The same sequence can then be called from another place in the program and afterward return to this second place.

The sequence of instructions which is accessed by the CALL command is referred to as a *subroutine*. This concept of calling a subroutine is used in many computer languages and may be familiar to some readers.

When a CALL instruction is executed, the contents of the Program Counter are pushed onto the stack. In this way, the location from which the subroutine is called is saved. The

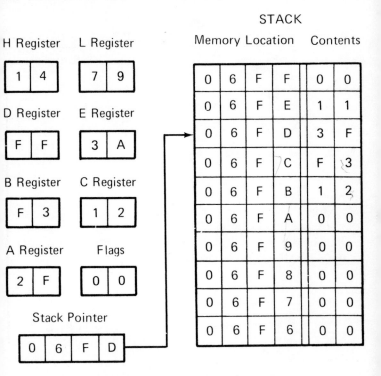

Figure 11.5   System status after the POP B command.

RETurn instruction causes the contents of the Program Counter to be popped off of the stack. The program flow then continues from the point of the subroutine CALL command.

Subroutines can also be nested. That is one subroutine may call another subroutine and so forth. This sort of operation can be continued to any level as long as the stack is large enough. Note that, whenever subroutines are used, it is necessary to initialized the stack pointer.

11.3 Example

For the example of Table 10.1, we will write a subroutine whose job it is to print on the teletype the character that is stored in register B. This subroutine will then be used in two places in the program.

The subroutine will be named TOUT and will be written as follows:

Name	Instruction		Comment
TOUT:	IN	1	;GET TELETYPE STATUS
	RRC		
	RRC		
	RRC		
	JC	TOUT	;JMP IF TTY BUSY
	MOV	A,B	;GET CHARACTER
	OUT	0	;PRINT IT
	RET		;RETURN TO MAIN PROGRAM

Note that this is essentially the same as the instructions beginning at LOP2 in Table 10.1.

To use this subroutine, we need to modify the program and include the subroutine as follows:

Name	Instruction		Comment
	LXI SP, 06FF		;INITIALIZE STACK POINTER
LOP1:	IN	1	;GET TELETYPE STATUS
	RRC		;PUT STATUS BIT IN CARRY
	JC	LOP1	;JUMP IF NO DATA
	IN	0	:INPUT CHARACTER
	MOV	B,A	;STORE IT IN B
	CALL	TOUT	;OUTPUT IT
	CPI	72H	;'CARRIAGE-RETURN'
	JNZ	LOP1	;JUMP IF NOT 'CR'
	MVI	B,8AH	;STORE 'LF' IN B
	CALL	TOUT	;OUTPUT IT
	JMP	LOP1	;START AGAIN
→	IN	1	;GET TELETYPE STATUS
	RRC		;PUT STATUS BIT IN CARRY
	RRC		
	RRC		
	JC	TOUT	;JUMP IF TTY BUSY
	MOV	A,B	;GET CHARACTER
	OUT	0	;PRINT IT
	RET		;RETURN
	END		

Note that the subroutine simply appears after the main program. It will be assembled along with the program and stored in the computer.

11.4 Exercises
This exercise will let you use a number of the features of your editor and assembler, as well as the CALL command. The objective of the exercise is to simulate a combination lock. In your program you should store a sequence of three characters and you will then have another person type three characters on the teletype. You will let him know if he has typed the correct sequence of characters.

It is strongly recommended that, in this exercise, you write subroutines both to read characters from the teletype and also to write them back on the teletype. The model given in Sec. 11.3 can be followed for outputting to the teletype, and a similar program will serve to read from the teletype.

Again in this exercise you are urged to think carefully of how you would structure this program before you actually begin to write code.

Your program should proceed in the following fashion:
1) It should read a sequence of three characters from the teletype. 2) If this sequence is not the "code word," it should output "carriage-return" and "line-feed." 3) If the sequence is correct, the teletype should ring its bell (perhaps several times), print "carriage-return" and "line-feed" and then turn on a light on the light and switch box.

If this problem seems difficult, you may wish to start by using a "combination" that is actually just a single character. If the problem seems too easy, you should write a program which will have the first user enter the combination, rather than have it as part of the original program.

12

MICROCOMPUTER ARCHITECTURE

In the previous chapters, we have placed primary emphasis on the software aspects of a microprocessor system. In the next several chapters, we will discuss the architecture or structure of a microcomputer system; we will be particularly concerned with methods for interfacing the microprocessor with other physical devices.

We have seen that the microprocessor can "talk" to many different devices: lights, switches, thumbwheels and terminals. These are only some of the devices with which it can interface; we will discuss several others in Chapters 13 and 15.

A simplified diagram of the 8080 system architecture is shown in Fig. 12.1. We have talked about some of this system before: the A bus, MD bus, D bus and DI bus. Here we have added more detail to the input/output (I/O) structure of the system. The CPU is actually several integrated circuits, including the 8080 chip.

12.1 Device Decoder

Let us consider first the operation of the *device decoder*. Remember that, whenever we did an input or output operation, it was necessary to supply a number to identify the particular device to be used: 02 for the Switch Register, 03 for the thumbwheels, 0B for the Light Register, and so forth. These numbers are called *device codes.* The purpose of the device decoder is to interpret these device codes and to make sure that the proper device responds. This is accomplished in the following way. Whenever an INput or OUTput instruction is executed, the device code contained in the second byte of the instruction is placed on the eight low-

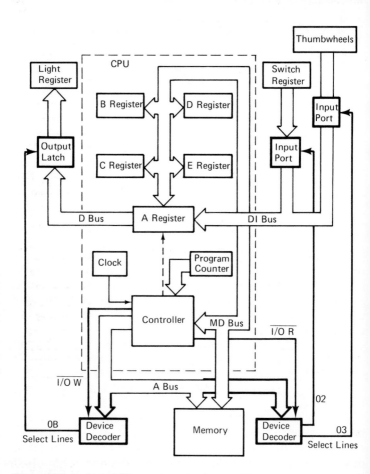

Figure 12.1 Input/Output control.

order bits of the A Bus. Either the $\overline{\text{I/O R}}$ or the $\overline{\text{I/O W}}$ signal is activated, depending on whether a Read (IN) or a Write (OUT) operation is to take place. Each of these signals is *active low:* that is, the signals become low (change from + 5V to 0V) when activated. The $\overline{\text{I/OR}}$ and $\overline{\text{I/O W}}$ signals act as general enabling signals for the device address decoder and keep the device address decoder from activating I/O devices during memory fetch and store operations which also use the A bus. In the simplest configuration, with only 16 device numbers, the device address decoder uses only the four low order bits of the A bus.

The device decoder, shown schematically in Fig. 12.2, is

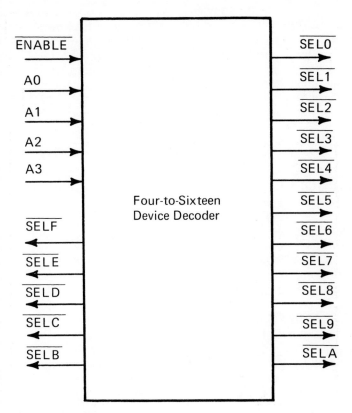

Figure 12.2 Device decoder.

nothing more than a four-to-sixteen decoder chip (Texas Instruments SN74174, for example). When the ENABLE signal is low, the four binary-coded inputs (A0 to A3) are decoded into one of sixteen mutually exclusive active low outputs (SEL0 to SELF). For example, if A3 to A0 are 0101 respectively, then SEL5 will be low, and all of the other select signals will be high. Note that A3 is the most significant bit. When the I/O operation is completed, the ENABLE line is deactivated (set to 5V) and all select signals become high again.

The structure shown in Fig. 12.1 allows us to have sixteen separate input devices and sixteen separate output devices. In this configuration, the same device code may be used for an input device and an output device, since the appropriate device decoder will be determined by whether I/O R or I/O W is activated.

It is also possible to use a single device decoder to select eight different input and eight different output devices. In this case, the $\overline{I/O\ R}$ and $\overline{I/O\ W}$ are ANDed together to form the $\overline{ENABLE}$ signal, and $\overline{I/O\ R}$ is used in place of the A3 bit. The first eight select lines will then be the input select lines while the second eight will be the output select lines.

An alternative approach is to use sixteen device codes but not permit the same device code to be used for both an input and an output device. In this case, the $\overline{I/O\ R}$ and $\overline{I/O\ W}$ are again ANDed to form the $\overline{ENABLE}$ signal, but the first four bits of the A bus become A0 to A3.

By the use of slightly more complicated logic structures, up to 256 input and 256 output devices may be employed.

The next step in the input/output process is to use the SELect line signal to generate either the input or the output. All output devices are connected to the D bus through *output latches* and all input devices are connected to the DI bus through *input ports.* In the normal state, these latches and ports isolate the devices from the busses; when a device is selected, it must be connected to the proper bus.

12.2 Latched Output

To output data from the microcomputer system, we use the *output latches* as shown in Fig. 12.3. Each latch is eight bits wide and is connected to the D bus. Each one has an active low select line input from the device address decoder. When a latch's select line is active (low), the eight output bits of the latch change (if necessary) to match the eight inputs from the D bus. When the select line becomes inactive, these bits are held (or latched) at their last value. Of course, this all takes place in a few microseconds. The result of selecting an output latch is, thus, to transfer the data from the D bus to the output of the latch. The data on the D bus was the contents of the A register when the OUT command was executed.

An output latch is actually nothing more than a set of eight flip-flops (Texas Instruments SN7475, for example). It is possible to connect many output latches to the D bus at one time. When an OUTput instruction is given, only the particular latch that is addressed by the device code of the instruction responds; all others continue to hold their current outputs without change.

12.3 Input Ports

Inputs to the system are accomplished by the use of an *input port* which consists of special binary logic devices

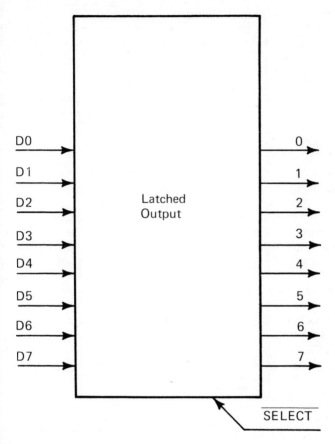

Figure 12.3 Output Latch.

known as tri-state gates. An input port is shown schematically in Fig. 12.4. As the name indicates, these gates are capable of being in one of three states: 1) A logical "one," 2) A logical "zero" and 3) A high impedance condition. In the first two states, the output of the gate matches its input. In the high impedance condition, the output is essentially an open circuit. Thus, it is possible to connect the outputs of a number of these devices together and, if only one gate is selected (i.e., taken out of the high impedance state) at a time, then the result will match the output of that gate. Thus, the entire device in Fig. 12.4 is essentially the same as a rotary switch.

The tri-state gates of an input port allow us to connect many inputs to the DI bus at one time. Groups of eight tri-state gates are connected to the eight-bit DI bus. When the

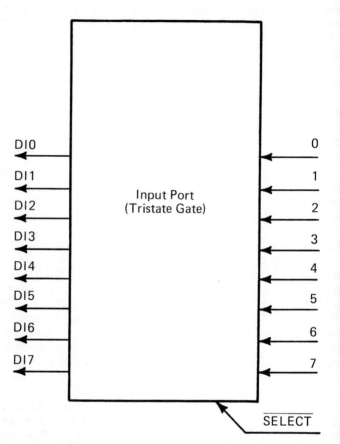

Figure 12.4 Input Port

select line for a particular group becomes active (low), its inputs are gated onto the DI bus and are then transferred to the A register by the INput instruction.

In some systems, the D, DI, and MD busses are combined into a single bi-directional bus. Note that the MD is already bi-directional since we are able both to read from and to write into memory. This combination has no significant effect on the structure discussed above since an output latch and an input port can both be connected to the same bus without affecting their operation.

12.4 Example

As an example of the use of input ports, output latches, and device decoder, we consider designing an interface for the light and switch box discussed at the beginning of the book.

We will use eight toggle switches for the switch register and eight light emitting diodes (LEDs) for the light register. Our objective is to connect the light register to the D bus when the computer executes an OUT 0B instruction, and to connect the switch register to the DI bus when the computer executes IN 02.

To keep the picture simple, we will use only one device address decoder and use the AND of the I/O W output and I/O R output as the ENABLE. Thus, we will activate the device decoder when we have either an IN or an OUT instruction.

The toggle switches that we will use are of the double pole, single throw (DPST) type. That is, the inner wire is connected to the selected one of two outer wires as shown in Fig. 12.5. The LEDs will be TTL compatible (see Chapter 13), and will have current limiting resistors as discussed in Chapter 13. The overall circuit will be as shown in Fig. 12.6.

When the CPU executes an IN 02 instruction, the low eight bits of the A bus contain 00000010 and the I/O R output goes low. Since I/O R goes low, ENABLE also goes low and the decoder decodes the low four bits of the A bus. Therefore, SEL2 goes low, but the other select lines stay high. This in turn enables the eight tri-state gates in the input port and thus the switches become connected to the DI bus. Those switches set to 5V will be read as ones and those set to ground will be read as zeros.

When the CPU is finished reading, the I/O R output returns to 5V. This disables the device decoder which then sets SEL2 back to 5V. Thus, the tri-state gates are returned to their high impedance state and the input job is finished.

A detailed analysis of the OUT 0B operation is left as an exercise.

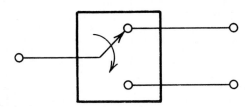

Figure 12.5 Double pole, single throw switch.

12.5 Exercises
1) Perform a detailed analysis of the OUT 0B operation for the example of Section 12.4
2) Modify the example of Section 12.4 to add another light register as unit 03 and another switch register as unit 0C.

3) Redo the light and switchbox example with both lights and switches as unit 00. Use only one 4-to-16 decoder.

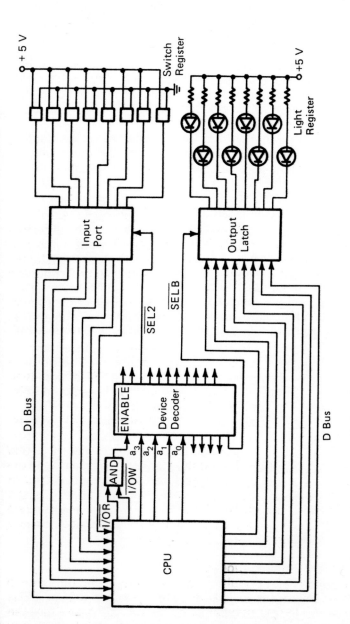

Figure 12.6 Light and switch box interface

13

INTERFACE DEVICES

In this chapter, we will discuss some of the input and output devices that can be used in conjunction with the I/O structure discusses in Chapter 12. There are a great number of such devices and new ones are being added constantly, hence, the list presented here is intended to be suggestive rather than inclusive.

Input and output elements of a microprocessor system are frequently described as being *TTL compatible.* This means that the voltages and currents required to operate the device are compatible with the requirements of conventional Transistor-Transistor Logic circuits. In other words, a "0" is a signal between 0V and 0.9V and a "1" is more than 2.4V but less than 5.5V. Generally, a "0" is considered to be 0V and a "1" is considered to be 5V.

Turning a TTL device "on" (i.e., making it a "1") can require no more than 40 μa (i.e., 0.04 ma), but turning it "off" may take up to –1.6 ma. The number of TTL devices that one device can control is called the "fan-out". Typically, one device has a fan-out of 10; that is, it can supply about 400 ma in the "1" state and it can absorb about 16 ma in the "0" state. TTL devices usually require a supply voltage in the range from 4V to 7V. The input ports and output latches of virtually all microcomputers are TTL compatible.

13.1 Light-Emitting Diodes
One of the most popular methods of displaying data from a microcomputer is with light-emitting diodes (LEDs). LEDs are available in a number of colors and sizes and have an essentially unlimited life. Their principal virtue is that they require only a relatively small amount of current. Therefore,

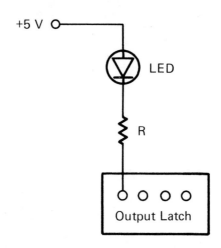

Figure 13.1   LED output.

they can frequently be connected directly to a TTL compatible output port.

Let us consider connecting an LED that requires 10 ma of current at a voltage drop of 1.7V. Our TTL output port can supply the needed voltage and current, but not both at the same time. Therefore, instead of turning the LED *on* when the output is a "1", we turn it *off.* You may recall that this was how we described the operation of the light and switch box in the early chapters.

We still are not done. Note that the LED requires 1.7V, but our TTL device has a difference of 5V between the "1" and the "0" states. Therefore, we have to use a *current limiting resistor* as shown in Fig. 13.1. For the present example, we want 3.3V of the total 5V voltage drop to appear across the resistor when 10 ma flows through it. Therefore, we use a 330Ω resistor. This gives us an output indicator that is *on* when the output is a "0", and *off* when the output is a "1". To reverse the output pattern, we would have to put an inverter between the output port and the LED.

13.2 Segment Displays
Single LEDs are convenient for displaying binary information. Frequently, however, one wishes to have the computer display numbers and/or letters. Grouping several LEDs together in the proper orientation makes this possible. The familiar numeric displays on calculators are actually just seven LEDs for each digit arranged in a figure eight pattern.

Figure 13.2 Fourteen-segment display.

Other arrays, such as the 14-segment pattern in Fig. 13.2, are also used. Seven-segment LEDs can be obtained either with or without a *decoder*. If the unit is not equipped with decoding logic, it will have seven inputs — one for each segment. The microcomputer must turn each segment on or off to form the desired character. The usual way to do this is to store a seven-bit pattern in memory for each character. When a particular character is to be displayed, the computer outputs the corresponding pattern from memory to an output latch.

If the LED is equipped with a decoder, the display needs only a four-bit input to specify which of the ten numerical characters to display. It uses the usual binary representation of each number from zero to nine and the code is known as BCD (binary coded decimal). Hence, two such units can be conveniently run from one eight-bit latch. The programmer would put the four-bit code for one display in the rightmost four bits of the A register and the four bits for the other display in the leftmost four bits of the A register before giving his OUT command. These devices are normally TTL compatible and, therefore, require minimal interfacing. They cost more than displays without decoders but, since they only require 4 control bits per character, they may reduce overall system cost.

13.3 Liquid Crystal Displays

Another type of display that is seeing increased use with microcomputers is the Liquid Crystal Display. (This is the same display used in those electronic watches that tell time rather than waiting to be asked.) Although liquid crystal displays change slowly (they require about 0.1 seconds), are somewhat temperature sensitive (they operate in the range 0°C–50°C), and are currently more expensive then LEDs, they have, nonetheless, two distinct advantages. They require very little power and they can be seen in strong light.

A seven-segment liquid crystal display is similar to a seven-segment LED display without a decoder, but differs in that it must be driven with a 5V square wave (30 Hz–100 Hz) rather than with a DC level. Therefore, the microcomputer must either switch the liquid crystal on and off every 10 ms or it must have a special clock to drive the display. Because of the added complication, liquid crystals tend to be used only where their low power consumption and high visibility are especially important.

13.4 Relays and Step Motors

Frequently, microprocessors are used to control high-power devices like motors and solenoids. There are many varieties of relays that can be used in conjunction with a microprocessor system to control these high-power loads, but *optically isolated relays* are particularly convenient. An optically isolated relay is actually an LED which drives a photosensitive transistor. Since there is no electrical connection between the diode and the transistor and since there is no mechanical switching, there is essentially no noise sent back to the computer from the relay. The control side of the relay is a diode and it is usually TTL compatible. Thus, it can be connected directly to an output latch. These relays can switch circuits that operate at up to 250 volts AC and which draw twenty or thirty amps.

Reed relays can also be used, but may require a higher driving current and, as a result, may require additional current amplifiers to buffer them from the computer. Some small electromechanical relays may be run directly from the system without an additional interface. Both of these types of relays currently cost less than optically isolated relays and can be useful for controlling small loads.

Step motors may also be conveniently used with a microprocessor system. These are electromechanical devices with digital inputs. With each pulse provided from the microprocessor, the step motor rotates one increment. In this way the microprocessor can easily and exactly control the position of a mechanical device.

13.5 Thumbwheels

We have seen in several of our discussions, that thumbwheels can be used as input devices for microprocessors. A thumbwheel is just a set of mechanical switches. There are numerous variations of thumbwheels and we will describe

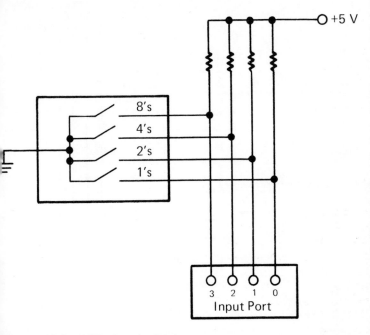

Figure 13.3 BCD thumbwheel.

only one. A *BCD-coded* thumbwheel is a ten position, one input, four output switch. Each output is either connected or not connected to the input, according to the BCD (Binary Coded Decimal) code of the switch position. For example, when the thumbwheel is set to 0, none of the switches are closed. When it is set to 7, three of the switches are closed and one is open.

When the switch is connected as shown in Fig. 13.3, the output of the thumbwheel can be directly connected to an input port. The resistors on the output "pull up" those lines that are not connected to the input by means of the switch setting. For instance, if the 1's switch is open, no current will flow through the leftmost resistor and the 0 input line will be read as a "1". If the switch is closed, current will flow and 0 input line will be read as a "0". Thus, the system shown will actually complement the thumbwheel reading.

Often one wishes to read many thumbwheels. The system shown in Fig. 13.3 could be replicated but it would require one four-bit input port for each thumbwheel. It would be desirable to reduce the number of input ports required. This can be done in a simple way by using select lines to "poll" each of the thumbwheels. The outputs of the thumbwheels

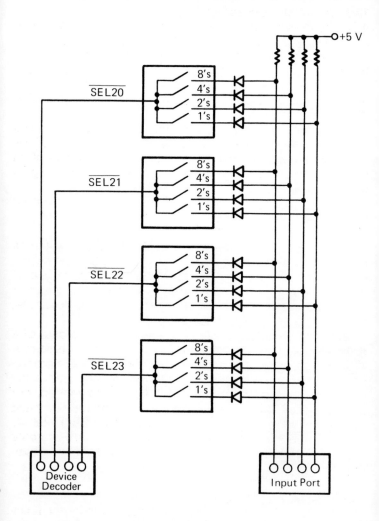

Figure 13.4   Four BCD thumbwheels on one input port.

are bussed together to a common input port with diodes used for isolation. Fig. 13.4 shows a possible structure for four thumbwheels which use BCD coding. A particular thumbwheel is read by setting the appropriate select line to the zero state; all other select lines are high. Therefore, the reading of only the selected thumbwheel is available at the input port. If electronic circuits interest you, you might wish to figure out why the diodes are needed.

13.6 A/D and D/A Converters

It is often desirable to have a microcomputer interact with an analog signal. For example, the computer may need to measure a voltage to determine a temperature during a control operation. Or, one may need to produce a voltage whose value is determined by the computer. These operations require the use of analog-to-digital (A/D) and digital-to-analog (D/A) converters.

A D/A converter is basically a series of resistors whose values vary be a factor two (e.g., 1Ω, 2Ω, 4Ω, 8Ω, 16Ω, etc.). By connecting each of these resistors to one of the bits of an output latch, an analog signal proportional to the digital signal is generated.

It is possible to buy D/A converters with built-in output latches. Such devices can be connected directly to the output bus.

An A/D converter is a more complex device. It measures or "samples," an analog signal and then, by using a countdown mechanism and a D/A, it matches the analog signal with an appropriate digital signal. The speed at which it does this matching is an important parameter of the device; the faster it is, the more it costs.

Although speed is a factor in determining the cost of a converter, it is not the most important one. The number of bits of resolution is much more significant. For microprocessor applications, eight-bit converters are frequently used. This means that the ratio between the largest resistor and the smallest is 128:1. Therefore, the large resistor must have a tolerance of 0.4%. If a six-bit converter were used instead, a tolerance of 1.6% would be sufficient. For some applications, twelve-bit converters are used. They require resistors 0.04% accuracy and are quite costly.

13.7 Exercises

1) How would you use a seven-segment display for hexadecimal data?
2) Can you write out the alphabet using the fourteen-segment display?
3) How could you read a set of eight thumbwheels using only one four-bit input port and one eight-bit output latch. Write a short program that would read the data and store it in memory.

14 INTERRUPTS AND REAL-TIME CLOCKS

14.1 Polling versus Interrupts

In many microprocessor applications, a number of input devices are connected to one computer. The computer must be able to receive input from any one of them but it can only be connected to one device at a time. There are two ways to solve this connection problem. Either the computer can ask each device, in turn, whether it has any input (i.e., it can conduct a *poll*), or it can let the input devices stop normal program execution when they have input (i.e., it can be *interrupted*). The polling method is easier to understand, but, it is generally is not the best solution.

The difficulty with polling is that it takes a lot of time. The computer must ask each device whether it has input often enough to be sure that it does not miss anything. Therefore, most of the time the computer will find no input and will have wasted its time. Although there are applications where this is not a problem, there are many where it is.

The use of an interrupt avoids the time loss inherent in polling. The interrupt capability allows an external device, such as any of our input devices, to directly affect the operation of the program. In this way, the computer can respond immediately to the external signal and then return to its main program.

14.2 Programming with Interrupts

At first it may seem that an interrupt procedure is quite complex; actually, it is not. If you do things in a logical sequence, everything works out correctly. In fact, the main program does not need to make any special provisions for being interrupted.

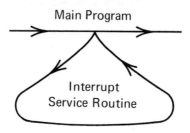

Figure 14.1 Servicing an interrupt.

The operation of an interrupt is shown diagrammatically in Fig. 14.1. The main program sequence is depicted as the straight line. When the interrupt occurs, the computer executes a short program to *service* the interrupt. For example, if an input device has data for the computer, it is read in and stored. When the servicing is finished, the computer goes back to the main program sequence.

If you think that the interrupt procedure sounds like a CALL instruction, you are right; it does. There are only three significant differences. The interrupt call:

a) is initiated by an external device

b) can transfer control only to one of eight memory locations

c) only requires one word of memory instead of three.

The eight possible destinations are all in the lower part of memory. Thus, even if your computer has limited memory, you can still use interrupts.

Since you cannot be certain where the computer will be when it is interrupted, you must be careful about how you start your service subroutine. For example, the main program may have been in the process of doing something in the A register. If you start your service routine with an IN instruction, you will destroy the contents of A. Therefore, before you do anything else in your service subroutine, you should preserve the contents of any registers that are involved. The easiest way to do this is with the PUSH instruction (see Chapter 11). Remember, however, that you must POP these registers back to their original values before you return to the main program.

One additional feature of an interrupt is that it "disables" further interrupts. That is, once an interrupt has occurred, no more interrupts will be recognized until the computer is told that it is all right to do so. It can be told this by having it execute the Enable Interrupt (EI) command. If you are using interrupts, it is a good idea to have an EI instruction at the very beginning of the program. That way, you can be sure that the first interrupt will be properly processed.

An interrupt is like a CALL command in that the contents of the Program Counter are pushed onto the stack before control is transferred. Thus, one would terminate an interrupt service routine with a RETurn command.

The 8080 system permits eight *priority levels* of interrupts; if two interrupts occur simultaneously, the one with the higher priority will be processed first. Each interrupt causes a CALL to a different one of the eight locations. It is possible to have an interrupt occur during another interrupt service routine. This does not pose any problem. In fact, we can nest interrupts just like we nested subroutines. This is illustrated in Fig. 14.2.

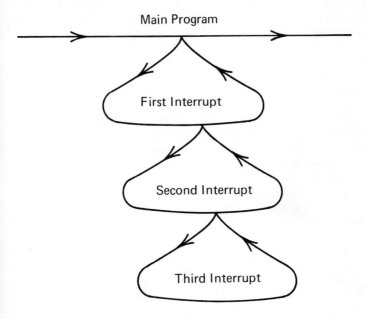

Figure 14.2 Nested interrupts.

14.3 Timers
There are many applications where a microcomputer must do something on a regular basis. For example, it may have to check the status of some measuring device exactly 1000 times each second. One way to do this would be to write a program that would take 1 m sec to execute. This "waiting loop" would be executed between each measurement. Un-

fortunately, this means that the processor can do nothing else.

There is another way. If one adds an external real-time clock to the system, interrupts can be used. Such a clock, or timer, is set to fire an interrupt at the appropriate time interval. Thus, the processor itself does not need to keep track of the time.

Some microcomputer systems are equipped with programable timers. This means that the user can set the interval between interrupts from his program. He can even vary the interval if he desires.

14.4 Example
To illustrate the use of interrupts, an example program that measures a temperature periodically will be presented. Suppose that when this temperature gets above a certain value, an alarm is to be sounded. Otherwise, the data is to be stored in memory for future processing.

This could be part of a fuel control system in an automobile. The cylinder head temperature is used to help adjust fuel flow and spark timing. If it gets too high, corrective action must be taken.

We will assume that there is an external timer that tells the computer when to measure the temperature. It does so by firing the interrupt which transfers control to location 0020. The service routine would look like:

Location	Code	Instruction		Comment
0020	F5	PUSH	PSW	;PUT A AND F ON STACK
0021	FB	EI		;ENABLE INTERRUPTS
0022	DB04	IN	04H	;READ TEMPERATURES
0024	FE54	CPI	54H	;COMPARE TO THRESHOLD
0026	F20638	JP	ALARM	;SOUND ALARM IF NEEDED
0029	320420	STA	TEMP	;STORE NEW TEMPERATURE
002C	F1	POP	PSW	;RESTORE A AND F
002D	C9	RET		;RETURN TO MAIN PROGRAM

Notice that we have shown the program as it would appear in the assembly listing. There is one instruction in this example program that we have not used before. After the ComPare Immediate, we do a JP. This stands for Jump on Positive, and it will cause a jump to ALARM only if the contents of the A register is greater than 54H.

14.5 Exercises

1) Suppose that when your terminal device is ready to print a character, it fires an interrupt instead of setting a status bit. Assume that the next character to be printed is stored in memory location 0600. Write an interrupt service routine that will output this character when the interrupt is fired.

2) In this exercise you are to write a simple traffic light controller. The lights at the intersection are all on output 03 and are connected as follows:

Bit No.	Lights
0	North - South green
1	North - South yellow
2	North - South red
3	East - West green
4	East - West yellow
5	East - West red

You have a real-time clock that fires an interrupt each second. The green light should stay on for 27 seconds and the yellow for 4 seconds. Assume that the interrupt fired by the clock starts you at location 0100. Assume also that the system has a reset to 0000 that you will use to initialize the program.

15 PERIPHERAL EQUIPMENT

In other chapters, we have discussed the use of terminals and the high speed paper tape punch and reader as input/output devices for a microprocessor system. In this chapter, we wish to consider briefly some of the other peripheral devices that one might use with a microprocessor.

15.1 Cassette Tape

The cassette tape deck of the type frequently used for music has been a popular I/O device for minicomputers for several years and is now being used for microprocessor systems. In some of the less expensive microprocessor systems, a simple inexpensive audio cassette tape recorder is used for this purpose. The more expensive digital cassette tape decks have the advantages of higher storage density (amount of information that can be stored on a single tape) and higher data transfer rate (the rate at which information can be written on, or read from, the tape). The two major advantages of the cassette tape as compared to paper tape are 1) higher storage density and 2) reusability of the tape.

In order to make effective use of a cassette tape system, it is necessary to have some type of Cassette Operating System (COS). A Cassette Operating System may be included as part of the system monitor or may be read in as a separate program.

The Cassette Operating System allows one to accomplish several tasks including:

1) Naming a file (program) on the cassette tape.
2) Locating a named file.
3) Loading a named (object) file into memory.
4) Writing a file onto a cassette.
5) Searching for free space on the cassette.

6) Searching to see if a given name has been used.

7) Deleting a named file.

8) Listing of files on a tape.

This sort of software support package is necessary because there is no simple method for a human to read what is written on the tape. The only alternative is to put each program on a different cassette. The above features are usually made available in a subroutine format so that they can be called by user-written programs. In this way the cassette system can be employed for storage or retrieval of data during the operation of a regular program. For example, a file of names and addresses might be placed on a tape for use in mailing promotional literature.

The cassette tape unit has two major disadvantages. Information is written on the tape in a sequential fashion. Hence, if one wants a program that is located earlier on the tape than the current position, it will be necessary to rewind the tape. This can take considerable time if the tape is long.

The second problem occurs if a single cassette tape unit is the only available high-speed, mass-storage unit. Consider, for example, the problem of copying a cassette tape. Each file must be read from the tape into memory, the cassette changed, and then the file written onto the new cassette. This means that each file must be short enough to fit into memory. This can lead to severe limitations on program length or large requirements for memory.

The operation of an Assembler in this environment can also pose a problem. Since the same unit cannot provide the source program and receive the object output simultaneously, it is normally necessary to use a one-pass assembler. This means that enough memory must be provided so that both the Assembler and the object program can be simultaneously stored. This can also be a severe limitation.

15.2 Floppy Disk

The floppy disk or diskette is an increasingly popular peripheral device for microprocessors. It was developed as a smaller and less expensive version of the standard disk device used on larger computer systems. It is called *floppy* because the storage media is a flexible disk of magnetic material. The price of the floppy disk system has made it competitive with paper tape and cassette tape systems. In addition, it has several advantages over these devices.

Because the storage method is magnetic, the small disk can be erased and reused many times just like the cassette tape. The disk itself look much like a 45 RPM audio record with a smooth surface and sells for about $5 to $10. Each disk can hold 250,000 to 500,000 bytes. Recall that a typical microprocessor system has only a few thousand bytes of memory. The data transfer rate of the floppy disk is also extremely high.

The major feature of the floppy disk system, however, is its ability for rapid direct access to information stored on the disk. It generally takes only a few milliseconds to find any one of the hundreds of programs stored on a disk. Contrast this to the need to find a paper tape (or cassette) and load it into the system and you see the reason why disks are so popular. The floppy disk system is particularly advantageous during program development stages, it can also be used in actual field operations if there is a need to access and/or store large amounts of data.

Disk systems are normally supplied with a Disk Operating System (DOS) which operates in a manner which is essentially identical to the Cassette Operating System. Note, however, that a single disk unit does not have the same problem as a single cassette. It is, of course, still difficult to copy disks. But the disk unit can use a two-pass assembler, since the source program can read from one place on the disk while the object output is written to another.

15.3 Line Printer

A medium speed printer operating in the range of 30 to 120 characters per second can be a useful addition to a microprocessor system. This is especially true if long programs are being written or if the system must output large amounts of data. The higher-speed printers operate just like the printer on a normal terminal but at a much higher data transfer rate.

15.4 Modem and UART

There are occasions when one wants to be able to access a microprocessor system by means of a standard telephone circuit. For example, one might want to retrieve stored data, check on operating status or supply information to a remote site. In order to accomplish this, one often makes use of a *modem* (modulator/demodulator) which allows the digital data to be transmitted over standard telephone lines. These devices transmit at rates of 100 to 2400 bits per second by converting the binary signals into audio tones.

Modems, as well as several other peripheral devices, transmit and receive data in serial form. By serial form, we mean that a byte is transmitted on a single line with the bits

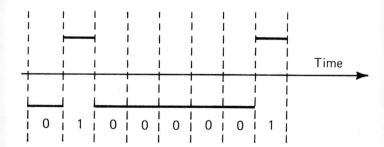

Figure 15.1   Serial transmission of the letter A.

following one another in time. This should be contrasted with the parallel form that we have previously been using where eight bits are handled simultaneously on eight lines.

Consider, for example, the transmission of the letter A, with an ASCII code of 41 (01000001), in serial form as shown in Fig. 15.1. Note that each bit is now assigned a specific time slot. The main advantage of serial transmission is that it uses fewer wires. For example, the serial transmission of the letter A illustrated in Fig. 15.1 uses only a single signal wire, while the parallel form would require eight signal wires.

The UART (universal asynchronous receiver/transmitter) chip is a convenient method for translating from serial to parallel and from parallel to serial data streams. The UART can then be connected directly to the DI and D busses. This is the method used to interface standard terminals. A UART is shown schematically in Fig. 15.2

The operation of a UART (General Instruments AY–5–1012, for example) is actually fairly simple. Basically, it performs three separate functions and acts as three distinct I/O units. These functions are:

1) Conversion of characters from serial to parallel form.
2) Conversion of characters from parallel to serial form.
3) Determination of the status of the UART.

The UART can receive serial data from a device such as a terminal and convert it to a parallel form to be placed on the DI bus. The serial data enters the UART on the line marked RECEIVE SERIAL DATA. Once a complete byte has been received, the RECEIVE DATA STATUS bit is set high to indicate that a character is available for transmission to the microprocessor. When the RECEIVE DATA SELECT line is activated by means of an INput command, the character stored in the UART is placed on the DI bus lines and inputted to

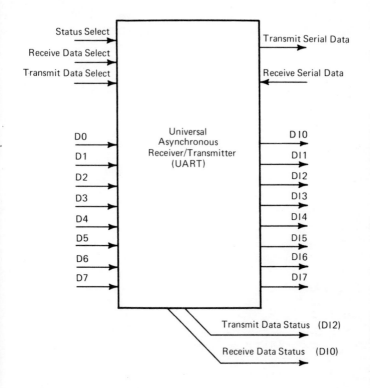

Figure 15.2 Universal asynchronous receiver/transmitter.

the A register. By varying clock rates and setting various parameters of the UART, it is possible to receive characters with several different formats and at various data rates.

The UART can also convert data received from the D bus to serial form and transmit it to a serial device. The character to be transmitted is placed on the D bus, and the TRANSMIT DATA SELECT line is activated by means of an output command. This character is absorbed by the UART and then transmitted in serial form on the TRANSMIT SERIAL DATA line. As soon as the character is received from the D bus and until it has been completely transmitted in serial form, the TRANSMIT DATA STATUS bit is high to indicate that another character should not be sent to the UART until it is free. Once again, the character format and transmission rates can be varied.

In order to determine the status of the UART, the STATUS SELECT line is activated by an input command. When this occurs, the RECEIVE DATA STATUS and TRANSMIT DATA STATUS bits are placed on the DI bus as shown in Fig. 15.2 and inputted to the A register.

15.5 Exercise
1. Draw a wiring diagram for connecting a terminal to the 8080. Include a device decoder and a UART.

16 COMPARISON OF VARIOUS PROCESSORS

Throughout this book we have been concerned solely with microcomputers which use an 8080 microprocessor. This is, in fact, only one of a large set of available microprocessors. In this chapter we will briefly review the major differences between the various processors. We should note that the technology in this area is changing rapidly and, by the time this is read, some of what is said here may have already become obsolete. Therefore, this chapter is not intended to be a complete comparison of *all* processors. Rather, it is intended to point out the *kind of differences* that exist.

The one characteristic which most easily differentiates the different processors is the number of bits per word. The 8080, as we know, uses an eight-bit word. Although this is probably the most common word length for microprocessors, it is not the only one. The first section of this chapter will deal with four-bit processors. These processors were the first ones on the market and were generally used to replace hardwired logic in fairly simple applications.

The next class is the eight-bit processor. We will briefly investigate a number of the more common eight-bit processors. Our objective will be to familiarize the reader with the possible differences between processors rather than to teach the details of each one. Finally, we will conclude with some remarks about larger processors.

16.1 Four-Bit Processors
The first microprocessor on the market was the INTEL 4004. This was a four-bit machine whose primary function was to replace hardwired logic in relatively simply applications. It was initially designed to be used in a hand-held calculator.

Since then, it has seen application in a wide range of areas. In fact, it is the "brain" in the Amana microwave oven.

The four-bit size is useful because this is the word length required to represent all ten decimal integers in BCD. In fact, each one of the sixteen keys on a simple calculator keyboard can be represented by a different four-bit string.

All microprocessors can be characterized by many numbers besides their word length. For example, the 4004 processor from INTEL can address sixteen pages where each page contains 256 eight-bit words; the I/O ports are four bits wide; the instruction set contains 45 instructions.

An improved four-bit processor from INTEL is the 4040. It is an upgraded version of the 4004 which responds to an additional 14 instructions. Also, it can accommodate interrupts which are not available on the 4004.

The detailed differences between these four-bit processors can be described at length. However, the major point to be made is that they are well suited to certain slow speed, low complexity operations where the cost of the chips involved is important. Their four-bit word length tends to make them more difficult to program than the eight-bit variety. As technology advances, the price difference between the four-bit and the eight-bit processors is shrinking. It appears that very few new designs will use four-bit machines.

16.2 The 8085
By this point, we are all fairly familiar with the 8080 microprocessor. A predecessor version, the 8008, is quite similar but cannot do all of the things the 8080 can. No new systems are being designed to include the 8008, but it is still used in some older products.

There are a number of integrated circuit companies which manufacture 8080 chips, and this processor has become more or less the standard by which other processors are judged.

The 8085 chip, introduced by INTEL, represents a continuation of the evolution of the microprocessor, From a software standpoint, it is essentially identical to the 8080. However, there are significant hardware differences. More elements of the computer system have been included on the CPU chip. Whereas an 8080 system requires separate circuitry for clock generation, system control and interrupts, these functions are all on the 8085 chip. In addition, the 8085 requires only a single 5V power supply, instead of 5V, 12V and -5V like the 8080. In addition, the 8085 runs 50% faster than the 8080.

The only difference in software between the 8080 and the 8085 is the inclusion of two new instructions in the 8085 instruction set. Both of these instructions relate to interrupts and they are included because the interrupt function is on the 8085 chip. Because these instructions use two instruction codes unused in the 8080, all 8080 programs can run on the 8085 without modification.

In addition to the new CPU chip, INTEL has also introduced new peripheral chips. These chips combine several functions, such as memory, I/O and a timer, on one chip and, thus, significantly reduce the number of chips needed for a complete computer. In fact, the basic system requires only three chips. The evolution from the rudimentary 8008, through the sophisticated 8080, to the highly integrated 8085, seems to indicate the direction of future microprocessor developments. Without significantly changing the logical structure of the machine, manufacturers are incorporating more functions on fewer chips that go faster and sell for less money.

16.3 The Z80
Like the 8085, the Z80, introduced by Zilog, represents an evolution of the 8080. However, instead of using increased integration only to reduce the number of chips in the system, the Z80 also uses it to increase the number of things the system can do. It has augmented the structure of the 8080 with more instructions, more registers and more addressing modes. It also runs up to twice as fast as an 8080.

The 8080 instruction set has 78 different instructions which use 244 OP codes. The Z80 has 158 instructions and utilizes 696 OP codes. The 80 new instructions include improved I/O, sixteen-bit arithmetic, block memory operations and more rotates and shifts.

In addition, the Z80 allows more flexibility in handling interrupts and it has more registers. It permits a number of different address modes which significantly improve programmability.

As an example of the increased flexibility of the Z80, consider the rotate and shift instructions. On the 8080, one can only rotate the A register one bit to the right or left and there is the option of whether or not to rotate through the carry bit. The Z80 adds the option of shifting instead of rotating (i.e. filling with zeros rather than doing an end-around operation) or, on a right shift, leaving a_7 unchanged. In addition, *any* of the standard registers or *any* memory location can be shifted or rotated.

This increase in flexibility applies to most aspects of the CPU. For example, one can set or clear any single bit in a register or memory; one can negate the accumulator; and one can do four-bit rotates between the A register and memory.

In general, then, the Z80 represents a significant step forward in eight-bit microprocessor sophistication.

16.4 The 6800

Perhaps the second most popular eight-bit microprocessor is the 6800 made by Motorola and others. It is similar to the 8080 but, in certain ways, it is more sophisticated and in other ways it is less sophisticated.

One major area of difference is that the 6800 permits additional methods of addressing data in memory that are not available in the 8080. For example, instead of having to specify the absolute address for a JUMP, one can simply jump forward or backward a given number of locations. Also, one can use *indexed* and *indirect* addressing. These are two addressing methods which may seem complex at first but can make writing programs easier.

Instead of a single accumulator like an 8080, a 6800 has two. The advantages of this should be obvious. However, it does not have auxilary registers like B, C, D, E, H, and L, and it must use its more sophisticated addressing capabilities to make up for this deficiency.

Like the 8085, the 6800 only requires a single 5V source. It would not be surprising to soon see an improved 6800-type processor that includes more functions on the CPU chip. It currently takes at least four chips to make a complete 6800 system, and a new generation will no doubt reduce this.

16.5 The F8

Another widely used eight-bit microprocessor is the F8 device introduced by Fairchild. The primary difference between the F8 and the other processors discussed so far is that the F8 contains more than just the CPU on its chip. This chip also has two I/O ports and sixty-four memory registers. When it is connected to the appropriate ROM chip, which also contains a local timer and two more I/O ports, one can build a very basic computer system with just two chips. The F8 represents a significant advance in the level of integration over the earlier processors and is a very attractive choice in those situations which require a small amount of memory and input/output capability. It does, however, require both 5 volt and 12 volt supplies.

Fairchild has announced two new versions of the F8 processor which are complete single-chip computers. The first combines the F8 CPU and 1K of mask programmable ROM on a single chip. This chip will require +5V and +12V power supplies. It comes in a 40-pin package, and 32 of these pins are I/O lines. Therefore, it is not possible to directly expand the memory of the device, and the user must be satisfied with programs no longer that 1K.

One difficulty with the F8 chip is that the ROM is only mask programmable. This could make system development and debugging difficult. To combat this, Fairchild offers an 'emulator hybrid" circuit. This is actually several chips on a single two-inch-square wafer that acts like the single-chip F8, but that uses standard EPROM chips. It can be plugged into the same socket as the single-chip device to check a program. When the program is correct, the mask programmed single-chip devices can be ordered.

A second single-chip system has also been announced by Fairchild. This device will have 2K of ROM and will require only a 5V supply. It is supposed to be available in late 1977 and will initially cost more than the 1K device.

16.6 The 8048

The INTEL 8048 microprocessor and its related chips are the first eight-bit processor system specifically designed for a single chip implementation. The basic chip contains a full CPU, 1K words of ROM, 64 words of multipurpose RAM, 27 input/output lines, and an internal programmable timer. Thus, by connecting a 5V power supply and a frequency reference (a crystal, a resistor and capacitor or an external source), one has a functioning computer. This is extremely attractive for those applications which use relatively short programs and limited I/O.

The 8048 family includes two other CPU chips. The 8748 has user programmable and erasable EPROM for its memory. This is very handy for prototype development. The 8035 has no program memory at all. It is well suited for use in a development system. As with most other processors, there is a wide variety of peripheral chips that can be used to expand the capacity of the basic system.

As one might expect, the increased level of integration must have some penalty. The logical structure of the 8048 and its instruction set are not as powerful as those found in multi-chip eight-bit systems. Thus, it can be harder to do some things. For example, there is no subtract instruction. Therefore, to perform a subtract, one must complement the subtrahend, add one to it, and add the result. This requires three instruction instead of one.

16.7 Other Eight-bit Processors

A number of other manufacturers make eight-bit microprocessors. Although this chapter is not intended to be an exhaustive survey of microprocessors, it seems only fair to include some mention of these machines. The fact that they are not discussed in greater depth does not imply that they are not useful machines.

RCA makes a microprocessor called COSMAC. The major difference between COSMAC and the others already described is that it is implemented in CMOS integrated circuit technology which means it requires far less power. There are some other distinct advantages. It operates from a single power supply having a voltage anywhere from 4V to 12V. Its clock can have a rate as fast as 2MHz or as slow as one wants. All of this makes it a very flexible chip that is well suited to those applications which use battery power.

The Rockwell PPS-8 microprocessor is essentially an eight-bit version of their four-bit PPS-4. The PPS-4 was originally designed as a calculator chip, and both processors are well suited to arithmetic operations. Rockwell offers a large variety of peripheral chips which interface directly with the PPS-8.

The Signetics 2650 is another eight-bit device. It too re-requires only a 5V power supply and a matching set of peripheral chips is available. Its instruction set permits indirect and relative addressing. Unlike the 8080, it has a *hardware stack.* This means that there is a special set of address registers on the chip that keep track of subroutine calls. This can be a nice feature in a system that only uses ROM memory. However, the stack can store only eight addresses so only eight subroutine calls or PUSHes can occur at one time.

16.8 Sixteen-bit Machines

The natural evolution from four-bit to eight-bit processors is continued with the sixteen-bit machines. There are, however, some differences. Whereas four-bit machines were quickly replaced with eight-bit machines, the same thing is not happening with sixteen-bit machines. The reason is that although the sixteen-bit machine is more powerful than the eight-bit device, it is not that much easier to use. The eight-bit processors are cheaper and are rapidly becoming well-known by system designers. Therefore, although sixteen-bit microprocessors will be extensively used, they will probably not replace the highly integrated eight-bit types.

Most sixteen-bit microprocessors are designed to emulate minicomputers. They can use the same software but are usually much slower. The correspondence between some minis and micros is shown in Table 16.1. The advantage of basing a micro on a mini is that all of the tools and expertise developed for use with the mini can be directly transferred to the micro. At least one device, the CP1600 from General Instrument, does not resemble an existing minicomputer.

A typical sixteen-bit application usually requires a fair amount of arithmetic capability. The longer word length in the sixteen-bit machine is well suited to both integer and floating point operations.

TABLE 16.1 Minis and Micros.

Minicomputer	*Microprocessor*
Digital Equipment PDP-11	Digital Equipment LSI-11
Digital Equipment PDP-8*	Intersil 6100*
Texas Instruments 990	Texas Instruments 990
National Semiconductor IMP-16	National Semiconductor PACE

*This is actually a twelve-bit machine.

17 OTHER APPROACHES TO PROGRAMMING

This chapter describes some of the other methods that one might use for programming microprocessors.

17.1 Cross Assembler and Time-Sharing
There are three basic methods for carrying out software developments for a microprocessor system:

(1) Resident Software
(2) Cross Assemblers
(3) Time-Sharing

We have been using a resident software approach in this book. In this case the microprocessor itself is used as the *host* for writing the software. This means that the system must have some form of editor and assembler that can run on the microprocessor system itself. It is an effective approach if only a small number of people are doing software development on one system and if higher speed input/output devices are available.

The *cross assember* approach makes use of a larger computer for software development. The cross assember allows the larger system to assemble programs and write machine readable output for direct entry to the microprocessor. If one has access to a larger computer, this can be an effective alternative to resident software. Often, the larger computer has a card reader and a high speed printer available which can facilitate software development.

The third approach is to use a time-sharing system for entry to a large computer with a cross assembler. In this approach, the microprocessor program is written and edited on a teletype which is connected to a large time-sharing computer facility. Once again the large machine then prepares a machine readable output for entry into the microprocessor.

17.2 PL/M*

PL/M is a high-level programming language developed by INTEL to simplify system programming for the 8080 family of microprocessors. Since PL/M is closely related to the popular PL/1 language, it facilitates the use of modern structured programming techniques. These techniques lead to rapid system development and checkout, straightforward maintenance and modification as well as a software product of high reliability.

The use of PL/M has several advantages for the system programmer. The programming takes place in a language which is more like ordinary English than is assembly language programming. PL/M also gives the programmer simplified control of the processor for the needs of systems programming but provides automatic control of many specific processor resources such as registers, memory and the stack. As a consequence, PL/M programs have a high degree of portability between systems.

A PL/M program is divided into *declaration* and *executable* statements. Declaration statements control the allocation of storage, define simple textual substitutions (macros) and define procedures. Since PL/M is a *block structured language,* procedures may contain further declarations which control storage allocation and define other procedures.

The procedure definition facility of PL/M allows modular programming: a program can be divided into sections (e.g., teletype input, conversion from binary to decimal forms, and printing output mesages). Each of these sections is written as a PL/M procedure. Such procedures are conceptually simple, easy to formulate and debug, and easily incorporated into a large program. They may form a basis for a procedure library, if a family of similar programs is being developed.

PL/M handles two kinds of data: BYTE and ADDRESS. A BYTE variable or constant is one that can be represented as an eight-bit quantity; an ADDRESS variable or constant is a sixteen-bit or double-byte quantity. The programmer can DECLARE variable names to represent BYTE or ADDRESS

---

*PL/M is a registered trademark of the INTEL Corporation.

values. One can also declare vectors (or arrays) of type BYTE or ADDRESS.

In general, executable statements specify the computational processes that are to take place. To achieve this, arithmetic, logical (Boolean), and comparison (relational) operators are defined for variables and constants of both types (BYTE and ADDRESS). These operators and operands are combined to form EXPRESSIONS, which resemble those of elementary algebra. For example, the PL/M expression $X*(Y - 3)/R$ represents this calculation: the value of X multiplied by the quantity Y-3, divided by the value of R. Expressions are a major component of PL/M statements. A simple statement form is the PL/M ASSIGNMENT statement, which computes a result and stores it in a memory location defined by a variable name. The assignment $Q = X*(Y-3)/R$ first causes the computation to the right of the equals sign, as described above, then the result of this computation is saved in the memory location labeled by the variable name 'Q'.

Other statements in PL/M perform conditional tests and branching, loop control, and procedure invocation with parameter passing. The flow of program execution is specified by means of powerful control structures that take advantage of the block-structured nature of the language. Input and output statements read and write eight-bit values from and to 8008 and 8080 input and output ports. Procedures can be defined which use these basic input and output statements to perform more complicated I/O operations.

A method of automatic text-substitution (more specifically, a "compile-time macro facility") is also provided in PL/M. A programmer can declare a symbolic name to be completely equivalent to an arbitrary sequence of characters. As each occurrence of the name is encountered by the compiler, the declared character sequence is substituted, so the compiler actually processes the substituted character string instead of the symbolic name.

After the PL/M program is written, it is *compiled* into a machine language program. Programs generated in this way usually require more memory then equivalent programs written in assembly language. Typically they will be 20% to 50% longer. Thus, the decision to use PL/M involves a trade-off between cost of programing and length of program.

A simple PL/M program is given in Table 17.1. This program inputs from the Switch Register and the Thumbwheels. If the two numbers are equal, the common value is outputted to the Light Register. If the two numbers are not equal, a zero is outputted to the Light Register thereby turning all lights on. An assembly language program which will accomplish the same function is given in Table 17.2.

TABLE 17.1 A PL/M Program (INTEL 8080 PL/M).

```
/*   A PL/M PROGRAM TO COMPARE TOGGLE SWITCHES AND
     THUMBWHEEL SWITCHES
*/
BEGIN:   THUMB  = INPUT (3);  /*  INPUT THUMBWHEEL*/
         TOGGLE = INPUT (2);  /*  INPUT SWITCHES*/
/*   COMPARE*/
         IF THUMB = TOGGLE THEN OUTPUT(OBH) =
         TOGGLE; ELSE OUTPUT(OBH) = 0;
         GO TO BEGIN;

EOF
```

TABLE 17.2 An Assembly Language Program.

```
;  THIS PROGRAM COMPARES SWITCHES AND THUMBWHEELS
            ORG     0
BEGIN:      IN      02          ;INPUT TOGGLES
            MOV     B, A
            IN      03          ;INPUT THUMBWHEEL
            CMP     B
            JNZ     NOTEQ
            OUT     OBH         ;OUTPUT
            JMP     BEGIN
NOTEQ:      MVI     A, 0        ;PUT ZERO IN A
            OUT     OBH
            JMP     BEGIN
            END
```

17.3 BASIC

The BASIC computer language represents a different approach to programming a computer than the ones we have discussed so far. It is designed to be easy for the user to understand and, as a result, it usually does not make very efficient use of the computer. Therefore, a program written in BASIC can take much longer to run than the same program written in PL/M or in assembly language. However, it is much easier to write a BASIC program, and it is much easier to run a BASIC program. It is easier to write because fairly complex operations can be written on one line, and it is easier to run because it does not have to be assembled.

Each line of a BASIC program can contain a complex expression. For example, to convert a temperature in degrees Fahrenheit to one in degrees Celsius, one would use the expression

$$10 \qquad C = (F-32)*5/9$$

The same program in assembly language would be far more complex. In addition to arithmetic expressions, BASIC allows logical comparisons and various forms of jumps.

BASIC was originally designed to be used on a time-sharing computer system. The objective was to develop a language that was easy to learn and easy to use. In addition, it was supposed to be "machine independent." That is, if you learned how to use it on one computer, you would not have to relearn it for use on another computer.

Although the designers of BASIC were not successful in making the language completely machine independent, they came close. It is usually possible to take a BASIC program written for one machine, make some simple changes, and have it run on another machine. Therefore, the user of BASIC can select a program from a large library of existing programs if it fits his needs.

It is interesting to see how BASIC differs from assembly language and PL/M. As we noted above, a BASIC program is never actually assembled. The source program, consisting of the ASCII representation of the characters in the program, is loaded directly into the computer's memory. Obviously, the computer cannot execute this program directly. Therefore, another program called the "BASIC interpreter" is also stored in memory. When control is transferred to the interpreter, it "executes" the BASIC program. It does this on a line-by-line basis. It interprets the first line of the program into a sequence of 8080 instructions. It then executes these instructions and discards the interpretation. It repeats the process for each succeeding line. Therefore, the complete program is never actually written into 8080 language.

The process of successively interpreting lines becomes very inefficient if a program does the same thing many times. For many hobbiest applications, however, this inefficiency may not be noticed. It may mean, for example, that the computer takes 0.5 seconds to respond to a move in tic-tac-toe rather than 0.05 seconds; not a big problem. Therefore, BASIC is quite popular in the home computer field.

A BASIC Program which will function the same as the PL/M Program of Table 17.1 is given in Table 17.3.

TABLE 17.3 A BASIC Program (ALTAIR Extended BASIC).

```
10    REM     A BASIC PROGRAM TO COMPARE
20    REM     TOGGLE SWITCHES AND THUMBWHEELS
30    REM
40    THUMB = INP (3)
50    TOGGLE = INP (2)
60    IF THUMB = TOGGLE THEN OUT (11) = TOGGLE ELSE OUT (11) = 0
70    GO TO 40
80    END
```

Appendix A.

Alphabetical Listing of Instructions

The alphabetical instruction listing in this appendix is intended to help the user figure out what the various instructions do. If you already know what the instruction does but you need the OP code, the functional listing in Appendix B will probably be more useful.

In order to simplify the listing, several shorthand conventions have been used. For example, many of the instructions operate on each of the registers. Instead of listing the instruction separately for each register, we will denote the register involved by the letter r. When we give the binary representation for the instruction, we will use $r_2 r_1 r_0$ to indicate the three-bit binary representation of r.

In addition to the individual registers, some instructions refer to the register pairs and the flags. We will also have shorthand for each of these. Tables A.1, A.2 and A.3 show the conventions we will use.

In the listing, we list the instructions alphabetically by mnemonic. For each instruction, a number of properties are shown. The second column in the table indicates whether the instruction requires 1, 2, or 3 bytes. When possible, the OP code is given in hexadecimal in the third column. For

TABLE A.1 Registers.

r	r_2	r_1	r_0	
B	0	0	0	B Register
C	0	0	1	C Register
D	0	1	0	D Register
E	0	1	1	E Register
H	1	0	0	H Register
L	1	0	1	L Register
M	1	1	0	Memory location addressed by HL
A	1	1	1	A Register

TABLE A.2   Flags.

f	f_1	f_0	
z	0	0	Zero flag
c	0	1	Carry flag
p	1	0	Parity flag
s	1	1	Sign flag

TABLE A.3   Double Registers.

d	d_1	d_0	
BC	0	0	BC pair
DE	0	1	DE pair
HL	1	0	HL pair
PSW	1	1	Program Status Word (flags)
SP	1	1	Stack Pointer

some instructions, the OP code actually contains data and the hexadecimal representation will depend on this data. Therefore, the fourth column shows the binary representation with an indication of where the data goes. The number of clock periods required by the instruction is shown in the fifth column. For some instructions, the amount of time required depends on whether a condition is met or on whether memory is referenced. For these instructions, two figures are given.

In addition to the carry flag and the zero flag mentioned in the text, the 8080 has three additional flags. The sign flag s is set to one when the result of an operation is negative. The parity flag p is set to one when the result of an operation contains an even number of ones. The auxiliary carry flag x is set when there is a carry from a_3 to a_4. Its principal use is with the DAA instruction. Some instructions affect the flags and some do not. Just which flags are affected is shown in the sixth column. Note, for example, that decrementing *any* register (DCR) affects the z, s, and p flags without necessarily affecting the A register.

The seventh column shows what the instruction does. For example,

$$r + A \rightarrow A$$

indicates that the contents of register r are added to the contents of register A and the result put in register A. We use capital letters to indicate the contents of each of the registers or register pair; lower case letters represent the flags. The notation used in this column is shown in Table A.4.

The final column contains a comment to explain further the purpose of the instruction. Additional notation is summarized in Table A.5.

TABLE A.4 Operation Notation.

→	Data on left replaces data on right
↔	Register contents interchanged
+	2's complement addition
−	2's complement subtraction
•	Logical AND
+	Logical OR
⊕	Exclusive OR

TABLE A.5 Other Notation.

(HL)	Memory location addressed by HL
W	8-bit argument
P	8-bit argument
D_W	Data on D bus when unit W enabled
DI_W	Data on DI bus where unit W enabled
y	One-bit data to compare with flags
SP	Stack Pointer − 16 bits
PC	Program Counter − 16 bits
a_i	i^{th} bit of A Register
r	Register identifier or 3-bit data for RST instruction
ℓ	Used to denote low-order byte of 16-bit register
h	Used to denote high-order byte of 16-bit register
x	Auxiliary carry flag
INTE	Interrupt enable flag

TABLE A.6 Alphabetical Listing of Instructions.

Instruction	No. Bytes	OP Code	Binary	No. Perio
ACI W	2	CE	1 1 0 0 1 1 1 0	7
ADC r	1	——	1 0 0 0 1 $r_2 r_1 r_0$	4/7
ADD r	1	——	1 0 0 0 0 $r_2 r_1 r_0$	4/7
ADI W	2	C6	1 1 0 0 0 1 1 0	7
ANA r	1	——	1 0 1 0 0 $r_2 r_1 r_0$	4/7
ANI W	2	E6	1 1 1 0 0 1 1 0	7
CALL PW	3	CD	1 1 0 0 1 1 0 1	17
Cf PW	3	——	1 1 $f_1 f_0$ y 1 0 0	11/1
CMA	1	2F	0 0 1 0 1 1 1 1	4
CMC	1	3F	0 0 1 1 1 1 1 1	4
CMP r	1	——	1 0 1 1 1 $r_2 r_1 r_0$	4/7
CPI W	2	FE	1 1 1 1 1 1 1 0	7

Flags Affected	Operation	Comment
c, z, s, p, x	$W + A + c \rightarrow A$	Add with carry immediate
c, z, s, p, x	$r + A + c \rightarrow A$	Add with carry - used for multi-byte arithmetic
c, z, s, p, x	$r + A \rightarrow A$	Simple add
c, z, s, p, x	$W + A \rightarrow A$	Add immediate
c, z, s, p, c = 0	$r \cdot A \rightarrow A$	Bit-by-bit AND
c, z, s, p, x, c & x = 0	$W \cdot A \rightarrow A$	AND immediate
none	$PC_h \rightarrow (SP-1)$ $PC_\ell \rightarrow (SP-2)$ $SP-2 \rightarrow SP$ $W \rightarrow PC_\ell$ $P \rightarrow PC_h$	An unconditional sub-routine call to location PW is performed
none	if f = y, execute CALL	Conditional call based on flag f. Full names: CZ call if z = 1 CNZ call if z = 0 CPE call if p = 1 CPO call if p = 0 CC call if c = 1 CNC call if c = 0 CM call if s = 1 CP call if s = 0
none	$\bar{A} \rightarrow A$	Complement A
c	$\bar{c} \rightarrow c$	Complement carry
c, z, s, p, x	flags changed	Compare - flags set as if command was SUB r
c, z, s, p, x	flags changed	Compare immediate - flags set as if command was SUI

TABLE A.6 Alphabetical Listing of Instructions (continued).

Instruction	No. Bytes	OP Code	Binary	No. Perio
DAA	1	27	0 0 1 0 0 1 1 1	4
DAD d	1	––	0 0 $d_1 d_0$ 1 0 0 0	10
DCR r	1	––	0 0 $r_2 r_1 r_0$ 1 0 1	5/10
DCX d	1	––	0 0 $d_1 d_0$ 1 0 1 1	5
DI	1	F3	1 1 1 1 0 0 1 1	4
EI	1	FB	1 1 1 1 1 0 1 1	4
HLT	1	76	0 1 1 1 0 1 1 0	7
IN W	2	DB	1 1 0 1 1 0 1 1	10
INR r	1	––	0 0 $r_2 r_1 r_0$ 1 0 0	5/10
INX d	1	––	0 0 $d_1 d_0$ 0 0 1 1	5
Jf PW	3	––	1 1 $f_1 f_0$ y 0 1 0	10
JMP PW	3	C3	1 1 0 0 0 0 1 1	10
LDA PW	3	3A	0 0 1 1 1 0 1 0	13
LDAX B	1	0A	0 0 0 0 1 0 1 0	7

Flags affected	Operation	Comment
z, s, p, x	If $a_3 a_2 a_1 a_0 > 1001$ or if x = 1 $A + 6 \rightarrow A$ Then if $a_7 a_6 a_5 a_4 > 1001$ or if c = 1 $A + 60H \rightarrow A$	Decimal Adjust Accumulator. If two BCD numbers are added, DAA adjusts sum to BCD form.
	$d + HL \rightarrow HL$	Double precision add
s, p	$r - 1 \rightarrow r$	Decrement register
one	$d - 1 \rightarrow d$	Double register decrement
one	$0 \rightarrow INTE$	Disable Interrupts
one	$1 \rightarrow INTE$	Enable Interrupts
one	— —	CPU stops until an interrupt occurs
one	$DI_W \rightarrow A$	Input - 8 bits of data read from input device W
s, p	$r + 1 \rightarrow r$	Increment register r
one	$d + 1 \rightarrow d$	Increment register pair d
one	if f = y execute JMP	Conditional JMP based on flag f. Full names: JZ jump if z = 1 JNZ jump if z = 0 JPE jump if p = 1 JPO jump if p = 0 JC jump if c = 1 JNC jump if c = 0 JM jump if s = 1 JP jump if s = 0
one	$W \rightarrow PC_\ell$ $P \rightarrow PC_h$	Unconditional jump
one	$(PW) \rightarrow A$	Load Accumulator Direct
one	$(BC) \rightarrow A$	Load A with (BC)

TABLE A.6 Alphabetical Listing of Instructions (continued).

Instruction	No. Bytes	OP Code	Binary	Pe
LDAX D	1	1A	0 0 0 1 1 0 1 0	
LXI d, PW	3	— —	0 0 $d_1 d_0$ 0 0 1 0	
LHLD PW	3	2A	0 0 1 0 1 0 1 0	
MOV r, r'	1	— —	0 1 $r_2 r_1 r_0 r_2' r_1' r_0'$	5
MVI r, W	2	— —	0 0 $r_2 r_1 r_0$ 1 1 0	7
NOP	1	00	0 0 0 0 0 0 0 0	
ORA r	1	— —	1 0 1 1 0 $r_2 r_1 r_0$	
ORI W	2	F6	1 1 1 1 0 1 1 0	
OUT W	2	D3	1 1 0 1 0 0 1 1	
PCHL	1	E9	1 1 1 0 1 0 0 1	
POP d	1	— —	1 1 $d_1 d_0$ 0 0 0 1	
PUSH d	1	— —	1 1 $d_1 d_0$ 0 1 0 1	
RAL	1	17	0 0 0 1 0 1 1 1	
RAR	1	1F	0 0 0 1 1 1 1 1	
RET	1	C9	1 1 0 0 1 0 0 1	

Flags Affected	Operation	Comment
one	$(DE) \to A$	Load A with (DE)
one	$PW \to d$	Double register load immediate
one	$(PW) \to L$ $(PW+1) \to H$	Load H and L direct
one	$r' \to r$	Move r' into r MOV M, M not permitted
one	$W \to r$	Move immediate
one	--	No operation
z, s, p, x	$r + A \to A$	Bit-by-bit OR
z, s, p, & x = 0	$W + A \to A$	OR immediate
one	$A \to D_W$	Output to device W
one	$L \to PC_\ell$ $H \to PC_h$	Place HL in program counter
one unless ss = PSW hen all	$(SP) \to d_\ell$ $(SP+1) \to d_h$ $SP+2 \to SP$	Pop double register off stack
one	$d_\ell \to (SP-2)$ $d_h \to (SP-1)$ $SP-2 \to SP$	Push double register onto stack
	$a_i \to a_i + 1$ $\quad i = 0 \ldots 6$ $a_7 \to c$ $c \to a_0$	Rotate A left through carry
	$a_i \to a_i - 1$ $\quad i = 1 \ldots 7$ $a_0 \to c$ $c \to a_7$	Rotate A right through carry
one	$(SP) \to PC_\ell$ $(SP+1) \to PC_h$ $SP+2 \to SP$	Unconditional return from a subroutine

TABLE A.6 Alphabetical Listing of Instructions (continued).

Instruction	No. Bytes	OP Code	Binary	Per
Rf	1	——	$1\ 1\ f_1\ f_0\ y\ 0\ 0\ 0$	5
RLC	1	07	$0\ 0\ 0\ 0\ 0\ 1\ 1\ 1$	
RRC	1	0F	$0\ 0\ 0\ 0\ 1\ 1\ 1\ 1$	
RST r	1	——	$1\ 1\ r_2\ r_1\ r_0\ 1\ 1\ 1$	
SBB r	1	——	$1\ 0\ 0\ 1\ 1\ r_2\ r_1\ r_0$	4/
SBI W	2	DE	$1\ 1\ 0\ 1\ 1\ 1\ 1\ 0$	
SHLD PW	3	22	$0\ 0\ 1\ 0\ 0\ 0\ 1\ 0$	1
SPHL	1	F9	$1\ 1\ 1\ 1\ 1\ 0\ 0\ 1$	
STA PW	3	32	$0\ 0\ 1\ 1\ 0\ 0\ 1\ 0$	1
STAX B	1	02	$0\ 0\ 0\ 0\ 0\ 0\ 1\ 0$	

Flags affected	Operation	Comment
ne	if f = y perform RET	Conditional return based on f. Full names: RZ return if z = 1 RNZ return if z = 0 RPE return if p = 1 RPO return if p = 0 RC return if c = 1 RNC return if c = 0 RM return if s = 1 RP return if s = 0
	$a_i \rightarrow a_i + 1$ $\quad i = 0 \ldots 6$ $a_7 \rightarrow c$ $a_7 \rightarrow a_0$	Rotate accumulator left and into carry
	$a_i \rightarrow a_i - 1$ $\quad i = 1 \ldots 7$ $a_0 \rightarrow c$ $a_0 \rightarrow a_7$	Rotate accumulator right and into carry
ne	$PC_h \rightarrow (SP-1)$ $PC_\ell \rightarrow (SP-2)$ $SP-2 \rightarrow SP$ $00r_2r_1r_0000 \rightarrow PC_\ell$ $0H \rightarrow PC_h$	Restart - A special purpose one-byte call instruction. Used primarily by interrupts
z, s, p, x	$A - (r + c) \rightarrow A$	Subtract with borrow
z, s, p, x	$A - (W + c) \rightarrow A$	Subtract with borrow immediate
ne	$L \rightarrow (PW)$ $H \rightarrow (PW+1)$	Store H and L direct
ne	$H \rightarrow SP_h$ $L \rightarrow SP_\ell$	Stack pointer set to HL
ne	$A \rightarrow (PW)$	Store A direct
ne	$A \rightarrow (BC)$	Store A in (BC)

TABLE A.6 Alphabetical Listing of Instructions (continued).

Instruction	No. Bytes	OP Code	Binary	Pe
STAX D	1	12	0 0 0 1 0 0 1 0	
STC	1	37	0 0 1 1 0 1 1 1	
SUB r	1	— —	1 0 0 1 0 $r_2 r_1 r_0$	
SUI W	2	D6	1 1 0 1 0 1 1 0	
XCHG	1	EB	1 1 1 0 1 0 1 1	
XRA r	1	— —	1 0 1 0 1 $r_2 r_1 r_0$	
XRI W	2	EE	1 1 1 0 1 1 1 0	
XTHL	1	E3	1 1 1 0 0 0 1 1	

Flags Affected	Operation	Comment
one	A → (DE)	Store A in (DE)
	1 → c	Set carry flag
, z, s, p, x	A - r → A	Subtract
, z, s, p, x	A - W → A	Subtract immediate
one	HL ↔ DE	Contents of DE and HL are exchanged
, z, s, p, x	A ⊕ r → A	Exclusive OR r with A
, z, s, p, & x = 0	A ⊕ W → A	Exclusive OR immediate
one	L ↔ (SP) H ↔ (SP+1)	Exchange HL with top entry of stack

Appendix B.

8080 Instruction Listing by Function

ACCUMULATOR		
ADD	B	80
ADD	C	81
ADD	D	82
ADD	E	83
ADD	H	84
ADD	L	85
ADD	M	86
ADD	A	87
ADC	B	88
ADC	C	89
ADC	D	8A
ADC	E	8B
ADC	H	8C
ADC	L	8D
ADC	M	8E
ADC	A	8F
SUB	B	90
SUB	C	91
SUB	D	92
SUB	E	93
SUB	H	94
SUB	L	95
SUB	M	96
SUB	A	97
SBB	B	98
SBB	C	99
SBB	D	9A
SBB	E	9B
SBB	H	9C
SBB	L	9D
SBB	M	9E
SBB	A	9F
ANA	B	A0
ANA	C	A1
ANA	D	A2
ANA	E	A3
ANA	H	A4
ANA	L	A5
ANA	M	A6
ANA	A	A7
XRA	B	A8
XRA	C	A9
XRA	D	AA
XRA	E	AB
XRA	H	AC
XRA	L	AD
XRA	M	AE
XRA	A	AF
ORA	B	B0
ORA	C	B1
ORA	D	B2
ORA	E	B3
ORA	H	B4
ORA	L	B5

ORA	M	B6
ORA	A	B7
CMP	B	B8
CMP	C	B9
CMP	D	BA
CMP	E	BB
CMP	H	BC
CMP	L	BD
CMP	M	BE
CMP	A	BF

ACCUMULATOR IMMEDIATE

ADI	C6
ACI	CE
SUI	D6
SBI	DE
ANI	E6
XRI	EE
ORI	F6
CPI	FE

OPERATIONS

DAA	27
CMA	2F

MOVE

MOV	A, B	40
MOV	B, C	41
MOV	B, D	42
MOV	B, E	43
MOV	B, H	44
MOV	B, L	45
MOV	B, M	46
MOV	B, A	47
MOV	C, B	48
MOV	C, C	49
MOV	C, D	4A
MOV	C, E	4B
MOV	C, H	4C

MOV	C, L	4D
MOV	C, M	4E
MOV	C, A	4F
MOV	D, B	50
MOV	D, C	51
MOV	D, D	52
MOV	D, E	53
MOV	D, H	54
MOV	D, L	55
MOV	D, M	56
MOV	D, A	57
MOV	E, B	58
MOV	E, C	59
MOV	E, D	5A
MOV	E, E	5B
MOV	E, H	5C
MOV	E, L	5D
MOV	E, M	5E
MOV	E, A	5F
MOV	H, B	60
MOV	H, C	61
MOV	H, D	62
MOV	H, E	63
MOV	H, H	64
MOV	H, L	65
MOV	H, M	66
MOV	H, A	67
MOV	L, B	68
MOV	L, C	69
MOV	L, D	6A
MOV	L, E	6B
MOV	L, H	6C
MOV	L, L	6D
MOV	L, M	6E
MOV	L, A	6F
MOV	M, B	70
MOV	M, C	71

MOV	M, D	72
MOV	M, E	73
MOV	M, H	74
MOV	M, L	75
—	—	—
MOV	M, A	77

MOV	A, B	78
MOV	A, C	79
MOV	A, D	7A
MOV	A, E	7B
MOV	A, H	7C
MOV	A, L	7D
MOV	A, M	7E
MOV	A, A	7F

MOVE IMMEDIATE

MVI	B	06
MVI	C	0F
MVI	D	16
MVI	E	1F
MVI	H	26
MVI	L	2F
MVI	M	36
MVI	A	3F

JUMP

JMP	C3
JZ	CA
JNZ	C2
JC	DA
JNC	02
JPE	EA
JPO	E2
JM	FA

CALL

CALL	CD
CA	CC
CNZ	C4
CC	DC

CNC	D4
CPE	EC
CPO	E4
CM	FC
CP	F4

RETURN

RET	C9
RZ	C8
RNZ	C0
RC	D8
RNC	D0
RPE	E8
RPO	E0
RM	F8
RP	F0

RESTART

RST	0	C7
RST	1	CF
RST	2	D7
RST	3	DF
RST	4	E7
RST	5	EF
RST	6	F7
RST	7	FF

INCREMENT

INR	B	04
INR	C	0C
INR	D	14
INR	E	1C
INR	H	24
INR	L	2C
INR	M	34
INR	A	3C

DECREMENT

DCR	B	05
DCR	C	0D
DCR	D	15
DCR	E	1D

DCR	H	25
DCR	L	2D
DCR	M	35
DCR	A	30

STORE/LOAD

SHLD	22
STA	32
LHLD	2A
LDA	3A

DOUBLE REG.

STAX	B	02
STAX	D	12
LDAX	B	0A
LDAX	D	1A
DAD	B	09
DAD	D	19
DAD	H	29
DAD	SP	39
XTHL		E3
PCHL		E9
XCHG		EB
SPHL		F9

CARRY FLAG

STC	37
CMC	3F

INCR/DECR

INX	B	03
INX	D	13
INX	H	23
INX	SP	33
DCX	B	05
DCX	D	1B
DCX	H	2B
DCX	SP	3B

ROTATE

RLC	07
RRC	0F
RAL	17
RAR	1F

DOUBLE REG.
IMMEDIATE

LXI	B	01
LXI	D	11
LXI	H	21
LXI	SP	31

CONTROL

NOP	00
HLT	76
EI	FB
DI	F3

STACK

POP	B	C1
POP	D	D1
POP	H	E1
POP	PSW	F1
PUSH	B	C5
PUSH	D	D5
PUSH	H	E5
PUSH	PSW	F5

I/O

IN	DB
OUT	D3

Appendix C.

American Standard Code
for Information Interchange.

The American Standard Code for Information Interchange (1968 ASCII) is defined by the American National Standards Institute in their publication X 3.4 – 1968. They describe it as follows:

"This coded character set is to be used for the general interchange of information among information processing systems, communication systems, and associated equipment."

The code is a 7-bit code which is used for upper and lower case letters, punctuation, special symbols and control characters. It is summarized in Table C.1. The table gives the hexadecimal form of each character. For example, the ASCII code for T is 54. Explanations of the non-printing characters are given in Table C.2.

There are four possible conventions for specifying the eighth, or most significant, bit of the character when an 8-bit form of ASCII is used. There is no standard for this bit and all four methods are used. The four methods and examples are summarized in Table C.3. *Even parity* means that the eighth bit is chosen so that each code has an even number of ones, while *odd parity* means that it is chosen so that each code has an odd number of ones. The *mark parity* convention always assigns 1 to the extra bit, while the *space parity* always assigns 0 to it.

TABLE C.1 ASCII Code.

Least Significant Character of Code

	0	1	2	3	4	5	6	7	8	9	A	B	C	D	E	F
0	NUL	SOH	STX	ETX	EOT	ENQ	ACK	BEL	BS	HT	LF	VT	FF	CR	SO	SI
1	DLE	DC1	DC2	DC3	DC4	NAK	SYN	ETB	CAN	EM	SUB	ESC	FS	GS	RS	US
2	SP	!	"	#	$	%	&	'	(	)	*	+	,	-	.	/
3	0	1	2	3	4	5	6	7	8	9	:	;	<	=	>	?
4	@	A	B	C	D	E	F	G	H	I	J	K	L	M	N	O
5	P	Q	R	S	T	U	V	W	X	Y	Z	[	\	]	^	_
6	`	a	b	c	d	e	f	g	h	i	j	k	l	m	n	o
7	p	q	r	s	t	u	v	w	x	y	z	{	|	}	~	DEL

Most Significant Character

TABLE C.2 Non-printing Characters

NUL (Null): The all-zero character used for time fill and media fill.

SOH (Start of Heading): Used at the beginning of a sequence of characters which constitute a machine-sensible address or routing information. Such a sequence is referred to as the "heading".

STX (Start of Text): Precedes a sequence of characters that is to be treated as an entity and entirely transmitted to the ultimate destination. Such a sequence is referred to as "text."

ETX (End of Text): Used to terminate a sequence of characters started with STX and transmitted as an entity.

EOT (End of Transmission): Used to indicate the conclusion of a transmission, which may have contained one or more texts and any associated headings.

ENQ (Enquiry): Used in data communication systems as a request for a response from a remote station.

ACK (Acknowledge): Transmitted by a receiver as an affirmative response to a sender.

BEL (Bell): A character for use when there is a need to call for human attention.

BS (Backspace): Controls the movement of the printing position one printing space backward on the same printing line.

HT (Horizontal Tabulation): Controls the movement of the printing position to the next in a series of predetermined positions along the printing line.

LF (Line Feed): Controls the movement of the printing position to the next printing line.

VT (Vertical Tabulation): Controls the movement of the printing position to the next in a series of predetermined printing lines.

FF (Form Feed): Controls the movement of the printing position to the first predetermined printing line on the next form or page.

CR (Carriage Return): Controls the movement of the printing position to the first printing position on the same printing line.

SO (Shift Out): Indicates that the code combinations which follow shall be interpreted as outside of the character set of the standard code table.

SI (Shift In): Indicates that the code combinations which follow shall be interpreted according to the standard code table.

DLE (Data Link Escape): Changes the meaning of a limited number of contiguously following characters. It is used exclusively to provide supplementary controls in data communication networks.

DC1, DC2, DC3, DC4 (Device Controls): For the control of ancillary devices associated with data processing or telecommunication systems, more especially, switching devices "on" or "off."

NAK (Negative Acknowledge): Transmitted by a receiver as a negative response to the sender.

SYN (Synchronous Idle): Used by a synchronous transmission system in the absence of any other character to provide a signal from which synchronism may be achieved or retained.

ETB (End of Transmission Block): Used to indicate the end of a block of data for communication purposes.

CAN (Cancel): Used to indicate that the data with which it is sent is in error or is to be disregarded.

EM (End of Medium): Used to identify the physical end of the medium, or the end of the used, or wanted, portion of information recorded on a medium.

SUB (Substitute): May be substituted for a character which is determined to be invalid or in error.

ESC (Escape): Intended to provide code extension (supplementary characters) in general information interchange. The Escape character itself is a prefix affecting the interpretation of a limited number of contiguously following characters.

FS (File Separator), GS (Group Separator), RS (Record Separator), and US (Unit Separator): These may be used within data in optional fashion, except that their hierarchical relationship shall be: FS is the most inclusive, then GS, then RS, and US is least inclusive. (The content and length of a File, Group, Record, or Unit are not specified.)

DEL (Delete): This character is used primarily to "erase" or "obliterate" erroneous or unwanted characters in perforated tape.

SP (Space): A normally non-printing character used to separate words. It is also a format effector which controls the movement of the printing position, one printing position forward.

TABLE C.3 Parity Bit Conventions.

Convention	Method	Code For A	Code For C
even parity	$b_7 = b_6 \oplus b_5 \oplus b_4 \oplus b_3 \oplus b_2 \oplus b_1 \oplus b_0$	41	C3
odd parity	$b_7 = \overline{b_6 \oplus b_5 \oplus b_4 \oplus b_3 \oplus b_2 \oplus b_1 \oplus b_0}$	C1	43
mark parity	$b_7 = 1$	C1	C3
space parity	$b_7 = 0$	41	43

Note:　$\oplus$　means modulo-2 addition:

$$1 \oplus 0 = 0 \oplus 1 = 1$$

$$0 \oplus 0 = 1 \oplus 1 = 0$$

Index

STEP BY STEP INTRODUCTION TO 8080 MICROPROCESSOR SYSTEMS

David L. Cohn and James L. Melsa

8080 INSTRUCTION SET

Most Significant Character / Least Significant Character

2 byte Instructions
3 byte Instructions

MSC \ LSC	0	1	2	3	4	5	6	7	8	9	A	B	C	D	E	F
0	NOP	LXI B	STAX B	INX B	INR B	DCR B	MVI B	RLC		DAD B	LDAX B	DCX B	INR C	DCR C	MVI C	RRC
1		LXI D	STAX D	INX D	INR D	DCR D	MVI D	RAL		DAD D	LDAX D	DCX D	INR E	DCR E	MVI E	RAR
2		LXI H	SHLD	INX H	INR H	DCR H	MVI H	DAA		DAD H	LHLD	DCX H	INR L	DCR L	MVI L	CMA
3		LXI SP	STA	INX SP	INR M	DCR M	MVI M	STC		DAD SP	LDA	DCX SP	INR A	DCR A	MVI A	CMC
4	MOV B,B	MOV B,C	MOV B,D	MOV B,E	MOV B,H	MOV B,L	MOV B,M	MOV B,A	MOV C,B	MOV C,C	MOV C,D	MOV C,E	MOV C,H	MOV C,L	MOV C,M	MOV C,A
5	MOV D,B	MOV D,C	MOV D,D	MOV D,E	MOV D,H	MOV D,L	MOV D,M	MOV D,A	MOV E,B	MOV E,C	MOV E,D	MOV E,E	MOV E,H	MOV E,L	MOV E,M	MOV E,A
6	MOV H,B	MOV H,C	MOV H,D	MOV H,E	MOV H,H	MOV H,L	MOV H,M	MOV H,A	MOV L,B	MOV L,C	MOV L,D	MOV L,E	MOV L,H	MOV L,L	MOV L,M	MOV L,A
7	MOV M,B	MOV M,C	MOV M,D	MOV M,E	MOV M,H	MOV M,L	HLT	MOV M,A	MOV A,B	MOV A,C	MOV A,D	MOV A,E	MOV A,H	MOV A,L	MOV A,M	MOV A,A
8	ADD B	ADD C	ADD D	ADD E	ADD H	ADD L	ADD M	ADD A	ADC B	ADC C	ADC D	ADC E	ADC H	ADC L	ADC M	ADC A
9	SUB B	SUB C	SUB D	SUB E	SUB H	SUB L	SUB M	SUB A	SBB B	SBB C	SBB D	SBB E	SBB H	SBB L	SBB M	SBB A
A	ANA B	ANA C	ANA D	ANA E	ANA H	ANA L	ANA M	ANA A	XRA B	XRA C	XRA D	XRA E	XRA H	XRA L	XRA M	XRA A
B	ORA B	ORA C	ORA D	ORA E	ORA H	ORA L	ORA M	ORA A	CMP B	CMP C	CMP D	CMP E	CMP H	CMP L	CMP M	CMP A
C	RNZ	POP B	JNZ	JMP	CNZ	PUSH B	ADI	RST 0	RZ	RET	JZ		CZ	CALL	ACI	RST 1
D	RNC	POP D	JNC	OUT	CNC	PUSH D	SUI	RST 2	RC		JC	IN	CC		SBI	RST 3
E	RPO	POP H	JPO	XTHL	CPO	PUSH H	ANI	RST 4	RPE	PCHL	JPE	XCHG	CPE		XRI	RST 5
F	RP	POP PSW	JP	DI	CP	PUSH PSW	ORI	RST 6	RM	SPHL	JM	EI	CM		CPI	RST 7